TRAVELS WITH HAFA

TRAVELS WITH HAFA

IN SEARCH OF OURSELVES

PETTIJOHN

TRAVELS WITH HAFA

In Search of Ourselves

ISBN 978-1-5445-1575-5 *Paperback*

978-1-5445-1574-8 *Ebook*

FOR MY DAD, JIMMY DARRELL PETTIJOHN.

CONTENTS

PROLOGUE

AFTER A BREAKUP, I ALWAYS CYCLE THROUGH THE same old playlists that remind me of different times in my life, and I eventually land on "Time to Move On" by Tom Petty. Then I decide to finally move on. Once I come to that song, it's like I've mourned enough with my regrets and emotions and have embraced either the excitement of moving on or the eventual necessity of it. In a breakup, it's easy to feel that no one quite as amazing will ever care about you in the same ways again, and there's a sense of accruing loss from that day forward without them in your life. For some reason, the song "Rich Girl" by Hall & Oates always ends up on that playlist too.

A few years back I had gotten married to, and promptly divorced from, a bewitching, vibrant Argentinian woman. The American dream. She was 22 and I was 26 when we eloped in Vegas. After we split up about two years later, my friend Nic de Castro sent me a few songs that went into the breakup comeback rotation. One was "Men and Coyotes" by Red Shahan, and the other was "Record Year" by Eric Church. Both of those songs helped me come back to life and made 2018 my *record year*. By record year, I mean that I traveled more, wrote more and enjoyed life more. It's hard to imagine yourself on top if you're always staring at the bottom.

A little more than halfway through 2019, I had just been through another breakup, and then this road trip idea materialized. All my breakups have been my fault, in one way or another. The woman always ends up getting fed up and leaving me. That's what happened again, and it sent me spiraling into despair. And that's what led to my wanting to get out of town, or that's what I told myself, at least. I was 31. I had been living in Los Angeles for over ten years and was having those kinds of thoughts: that my latest ex was the one I'd been waiting for all that time. Now that it was over, most things seemed pointless. And many things were painful. I felt like I had nothing to lose and no reason to stay.

Getting out of the city to think about life and explore the Pacific Northwest became romanticized in my mind the more I thought about it. I had been stuck in a rut and routine that working from home just wasn't going to solve. My ex and I had been dating for about a year and broke up that August. So I spent September of 2019 reeling in that familiar self-loathing until Tom Petty started screaming at me to move on. I targeted October as the month to take a road trip. I told others that I wanted to get out of town and clear my head and find some perspective, which was all basically true.

Over the past few years I'd taken several extended trips to exotic places and countries, some by myself and some with other people. But now I had a young pup that was in need of training and attention, so I focused my planning on the type of trip where he could join me. I started researching different types of motor homes and bought a large map of the United States and hung it on the wall behind my desk at home so that I'd see it each day and begin to subconsciously design my route. As an American, born in Oklahoma on the Fourth of July, it seemed a shameful error that there was so much of my own country I hadn't yet seen.

On top of my headaches over the dissolved relationship, one of my neighbors had recently become a consistent pain in my ass. I'd lived at my house for seven years, and she had been there for two, living above the garage in a small studio in the backyard. Suddenly, if I smoked in the backyard, she'd complain. If my dog peed in the backyard, she'd complain. If I sprayed disinfectant and deodorizers in the backyard to get rid of the pee smell, she'd complain about that. I hate it when people complain about both the problem *and* the solution.

One day my neighbor came down her stairs in the backyard and Hafa ran up to her innocently to say hi, and the neighbor, panic-stricken, went, "He bit my shoe."

I had watched him carefully, and he clearly had mouthed and licked her shoe, but there was no bite. "Excuse me?"

"He made my shoe wet." She said it like she was due a serious apology.

I rolled my eyes as dramatically as I could. "Okay..."

What made it all the more aggravating, I'll admit, is that the neighbor in question was a petite blonde Russian. And Russians, or at least the representation of their corrupt government that we tend to hear about, seem to be the embodiment of Americans' natural and mortal enemy, in movies and recent election news alike. The idea of an oppressive regime sending out its brethren to the United States simply to impede my own sense of liberty offended me at my core.

I work with several friendly Russians too, who are great people, and I don't want to generalize, but this neighbor of mine was so wound up. It was as though she spent her days staring out the window into the backyard looking for reasons to be upset. Her complaints were always dramatized to an extent that you'd think breaking her strict rules was the worst possible offense. She was protective and aggressive about what I could do in my own backyard. I was on the verge of putting up a suggestion box by my back door for her to simply drop in some carefully typed notes of rules and citations so that I could direct her to the box rather than having daily confrontations.

I live in Hermosa Beach, California in LA County. Hermosa is 6 miles south of the LAX airport and makes up about 2 square miles, packed densely with the homes and apartments of its 20,000 or so residents. My place is a cute classic home built about 100 years ago, a block from the beach. The community is safe and clean, with a focus on being outdoors, surfing, playing volleyball, those types of activities. Many people in my neighborhood refer to the South Bay as "the bubble," since it's far enough away from the craziness of the city of LA to be quiet, but close enough to be able to commute for work, meetings or events. While Santa Monica and Venice are overrun with tourists, a half-hour south in Hermosa it's much calmer, cleaner and mostly locals on the beach. It's a bit less exciting than those parts of town and is what you could consider kind of vanilla.

Because I make all of my income remotely, little was stopping me from leaving town—even finances, however shaky they were at the time. I've never been great at saving money or spending it wisely. If there is more revenue one month, I'll invest it into some other part of my business or use it toward a trip. My life doesn't require a lot of overhead, but if I need to put something on credit to make a trip happen, I'm not the type to hesitate or consider future implications. I have no assets, no savings and few investments. I haven't even owned a car in the last five years. Aside from my dog, I have little tying me down.

I have tried to adapt my own philosophy as a generous interpretation of the Osho quote, "I live my life based on two principles. One, I live as if today was my last day on earth. Two, I live today as if I am going to live forever."

MAKING A PLAN

BY MID-SEPTEMBER I STARTED VISITING RV RENTAL places in the South Bay to walk around and see the rigs up close, touch them, poke around inside and imagine how much room would be required for me and the dog.

My dog's name is Raphael. He's a German shepherd that I've raised in LA with a Brazilian name, and I've taught him some basic commands in Portuguese. He knows that *senta* means "sit," *venha aqui* means "come here," and *deitar* means "lie down." He knows a few phrases in English too, like "drop it," but the idea was to purposefully teach him in another language so he'd only listen to me when we're in the States. Most experts in this field, whoever they may be, say that smart dogs can learn over 150 words, and some say they can learn even more than that. I only know a handful of phrases in Portuguese myself, but I say them to him and assume he understands. I'll say things like *bon dia* for "good morning," *bon garato* for "good boy" and *obrigado* for "thank you." Brazilians pronounce their Rs like Hs, which makes his real name sound like Haphael. Shortened it's just Rafa and sounds like Hoffa, so I spell it here as Hafa.

Hafa was nearly nine months old when we took this road trip, and I was still in the midst of training him. Even at that age, he was already nearing 80 pounds and was an intimidating presence. German shepherds are such small, cute puppies until around six months old, and then they get big fast. He's a red-and-black shepherd; his dad was from Germany and weighed over 95 pounds. In fact, his dad, called a "sire" in breeding terms, was named Isko Vom Spessartblick. How's that for a real German name for a German dog? Hafa has his papers as a champion breed dog, and I got him when he was eight weeks old. He was and is still growing every day. He's always had big paws and pointy ears, and when he's tired or happy, his tongue extends out of his mouth by 3 or 4 inches. It's a massive tongue, and when he's lying outside on the ground after playing fetch, it will hang out of his mouth, resting on the grass like a piece of Laffy Taffy as he pants away in a sort of exhausted ecstasy.

When I first got Hafa, I hired a dog trainer named Brian Lee. His company is called Way of the Dog, and he's been recognized as a top dog trainer in my neighborhood for years. I also took Hafa to some obedience and agility training classes at another place nearby, called Zoom Room, but Brian took me step-by-step on training Hafa from the time he was two months old. I've had other great dogs in the past, but I learned a tremendous amount from Brian in our sessions. He'd say, "If you put the time in for the first two years, you'll then have a perfect dog for the next 12 to 14 years."

I'd complain about something, like how Hafa wouldn't bring tennis balls back to me when we were playing fetch, and Brian would tell me to bring several balls to the park instead of one and to keep throwing them. I did that, and now when we play fetch I only need one ball because Hafa has learned to bring it back to me. I told Brian how Hafa would hide tennis balls under my couch and then scratch at the foot of the couch to get them out, and Brian would suggest I block off the bottom of the couch with some wood, or get a different couch that didn't have that size opening near the floor. "Just remove the ability for him to do that." A sort of judo, "Solve the problem before it starts"-type of philosophy. Then I told him that I'd snapped at Hafa for chewing up my flip-flops and my phone charger, and Brian told me not to punish the dog for those kinds of things. He'd say it was my fault for leaving those belongings on the ground where the dog could find them in the first place, and then he'd say something to me like, "If you wanted a stuffed animal, you should have bought a stuffed animal. You have a puppy, and he's being a puppy." In his view, you should only punish a dog for barking, biting or jumping on someone.

There were three main rules Brian insisted on from the day I first met him. Rule one: that the dog has access to me at night. This doesn't mean the dog has to be allowed on the bed, but it does mean that he's able to at least see the bed at night. Dogs are pack animals and want to be able to sleep nearby, whether in a dog bed in the bedroom or in some area where they can at least see the bed if they want to. Rule two: that the dog is always allowed to roam around in the house, and is never locked in a closet or something. This seems like it would be obvious, but for some people it isn't. Rule three: the five-hour rule. You can't leave the dog alone by itself for more than five hours. Someone must take it for a walk and let it out at least every five hours during the day.

Brian, and all the dog-training books I had read, insisted on crate training as well, but I never bothered with that. Since I didn't use a crate, potty training was a mess and a headache, but we got through it. I've dabbled in some scent training in order to teach him how to find certain things with his virtuosic nose, but he still has a long way to go. I would love someday to teach him how to find crisp, fresh $100 bills. Hafa at least knows the obedience basics in some combination of English and Portuguese, and he's never been mean or aggressive. He's still a young pup, but he's sweet and friendly, and he loves to run up and say hello to people and other dogs anytime he's allowed.

Early on, I put specific rules in place for Hafa, like having to sit and wait before eating his food. Some dogs will charge their food bowl as soon as it's being filled and I didn't want that, so Hafa knows to sit patiently as I fill his food bowl, and once I say, "Okay," he knows he is allowed to eat. A few times, I've poured his food and gone about my day for a while before noticing, maybe 30 minutes later, that he's still sitting and staring at his bowl, waiting for permission. I'll apologetically say, "Okay, you can eat," and then he'll dive in.

Since it was just the two of us, we could fit in a Sprinter van or something else simple and practical. There are some cool decked-out Sprinter vans nowadays that you can easily find for rentals or to purchase, and I have nothing against that. I was mostly concerned with having a nice big bed and a shower, so not most people's idea of rugged camping by any means. You can tow Airstreams and trailers with a truck or Jeep and park the rig at a campsite, and then navigate the tougher roads in your main vehicle. There are a number of options available to road warriors and digital nomads, but I wanted something big, self-contained and comfortable.

As far as rentals go, there are some companies that have fleets of identical RV models with cheap-looking wood paneling and thin springy mattresses and no character. Just different lengths. I went to one such lot and couldn't leave quickly enough. There was another RV rental place not far from my home, and I discovered that they had an entire RV park with over 300 residents in the back of their shop behind a wooden gate. A small community of people living in RVs that I had been completely unaware of, a short drive from my home and hidden behind a fence that I'd never noticed. A little city within a city. That place had an interesting selection of chariots and decent pricing, but the rigs weren't very clean and I went home unfulfilled.

I ended up booking an RV from an individual who was listing his 2004 Fleetwood Southwind for rent on a website that facilitates renting directly from RV owners. The Fleetwood Southwind is among the most popular motor home models on the road today and is more affordable to purchase than I had first realized, at somewhere around $30,000 all in for that particular year and model. Buying one to list on one of those RV rental websites wouldn't be a terrible idea, as you can use the rig whenever you want and pay off its initial cost within the first year or two from the rental income.

I considered a few different models for the rental but chose the Southwind because it seemed safe and reliable for a long-haul trip. The owner of the RV I booked went by the name OB, and he had outfitted and customized his Southwind with an upgraded power system for an additional air conditioner. He had also put in a newer TV and satellite, a nicer bed and many other trappings of creature comforts. It was decorated with little knickknacks that made it feel more like a real home, like a little sign above the kitchen table that said, "Our Happy Place." At 36 feet long, the Southwind is the equivalent of a bus. Once I started looking at rigs, I found that anything longer than 36 feet seemed like overkill, but anything shorter was just a big van. Longer rigs do present some parking limitations, and there are many great remote campsites that you really need some sort of Jeep or four-wheel drive SUV to get to, places that you could never reach in a large motor home.

I only made two campsite reservations ahead of time. I'd decided that I would allow myself to find a place to sleep each night as though I were letting those places simply find me when I was tired of driving and content to park. When in doubt, make only the most critical arrangements and leave the rest to fate.

The two reservations that I did make ahead of time were for the first night in Zion National Park at South Campground, and one in Ashford, Washington at a spot called Mounthaven Resort for two nights, two weeks later. My rationale for the first campground booking was that I could have a spot for certain to rest after the first leg of the trip and would be able to comfortably set up the rig for the first time without the stress of also finding a place to camp. Since I knew that I would be boondocking a lot and couldn't predict how busy of a season October would make impromptu campground stops along the way, I wanted a midway point in Washington where I knew I could fill up on water and propane and empty the tanks and such. Having a halfway point chosen ahead of time would also help keep me on schedule to return the rig on time.

The year before, I had been to Montana with my friend Nic and our friends Rich and Erik. On that trip, Nic showed us some of his Montana. We camped out and he taught us how to fly fish. We even went to see Red Shahan play "Men and Coyotes" at Live From The Divide in Bozeman on that trip. Nic had since moved from NYC to Bozeman with his fiancée, Jentry, and they'd had a baby. So Bozeman became a figurative pin in the map as a destination for me to reach to go see them and meet their child. I told my big brother, Aaron, about the idea of the trip and invited him to join me for a few days, as the first few days of my journey would overlap with his birthday on October 6. I gave him a few options of ways we could make it work, and then, just like that, he said yes.

Aaron said he would plan to take a Thursday and Friday off work and drive up to my house from San Diego on Wednesday night after work, so that we could drive through the night and enjoy the first few days of the trip together before he flew home on Sunday from whatever city we ended up getting to by then. He needed to be back home in time to go to work on Monday. I had made the request for him to join me without fully thinking he would. By some manner of timing and luck, it worked out. Since he and his wife had moved to San Diego, we would often say how "we should" go and do lots of things together, but this time we made the time for it. I had also suggested to two of my friends, Rich and Zach, to pop in some weekend, but my brother was the only person to say yes. My ex-girlfriend and I even talked one night about her possibly joining for a portion of the trip, but she backed out the next day when she was sober.

Now that I knew Aaron would accompany me for the first days, I felt more at ease about handling this giant vehicle on the road and learning how to operate it. With my brother there, I was confident we'd figure it all out. Then I refined the routes. The Grand Canyon would be a logical place to start, since it's eight hours from LA and neither of us had been there before. But we also wanted to see the Zion National Park area, and I only had him from Wednesday night until Sunday night. Instead of rushing through several areas, we nixed the Grand Canyon entirely and decided to drive straight through to Zion from my house in Hermosa.

I figured that we could go through Provo and Salt Lake City from Zion on the way toward Montana, since our nephew Blake lived in Provo with his wife, and Salt Lake City would be a large enough airport for Aaron to fly out from on Sunday night back to San Diego. And like that, I had the makings of a plan.

PREPARING TO LEAVE

WITH THE RV AND TWO CAMPGROUNDS BOOKED, I still had about ten days to prep and buy groceries and supplies for the trip. I preemptively bought Aaron a first-class plane ticket from Salt Lake City to San Diego to surprise him with, as he'd be flying home on his birthday. Then I bought a mobile hotspot, so that I could have internet access anywhere along the way, allowing me to work on the move. I started stocking up on groceries and dog treats, and began researching some of the states I'd be passing through. I had envisioned going in a big loop, from Montana through Idaho and Washington, then back down south through Oregon and back to California.

I only had three and a half weeks booked with the RV and wanted to avoid feeling rushed at any point along the way. I will say up front that I still felt rushed throughout the trip and easily could have spent twice as much time to explore the same amount of land, if only I could have afforded the rental for more than three weeks. I'll overextend myself and my credit on a whim for a taste of adventure, but only about as far as I think is manageable.

When I picked up the Southwind that Wednesday, I drove her back home on the side streets rather than jumping straight on the highway, wanting to get a feel for maneuvering the monstrous machine. I stayed focused on the road and while I didn't turn the radio on during the short drive back to my house, I did keep singing Willie Nelson's "On The Road Again" to myself repeatedly in giddy anticipation. I'd finish singing it, then start right back up. "I just can't wait to get on that road again..."

Before picking up the RV, I had coordinated with two of my friends to park their cars in the two metered spaces right in front of my home in order to save them. Like clockwork, as I pulled up to my spot in Hermosa Beach, they moved their cars and I pulled in smoothly, with the bus perfectly filling the length of the two parking spaces. I later learned that I could have gotten a day pass from the city to park a large vehicle there. City parking enforcement being who they are, the rig was quickly ticketed, and then given another ticket for being an oversized vehicle on top of the first ticket. I left the tickets on the windshield as I loaded it up, hoping that would prevent them from leaving a few more citations for good measure.

Aaron said that he'd get to my house around 8 p.m., so I spent the afternoon loading the RV up with all the supplies I figured would be essential. In terms of food, I packed canned beans, pasta sauce, pasta, rice, popcorn, cheese, eggs, fresh vegetables, steaks, bread, turkey, onions, peppers and everything else that seemed relevant, such as bottled water, soap, paper towels, toilet paper, toothpaste and other basics.

My neck has had issues ever since a car wreck years ago that caused two degenerated discs, so I packed a cold pack and CBD pain creams for the trip, as well as two foam rollers and two lacrosse balls I put under my back and shoulders and roll around on. I packed skis just in case. I brought my chessboard and some other board games and playing cards. I packed a guitar, even though I don't know how to play. I packed way too many things and, still, I wished there was some way to fit my paddleboard too, as I was going to see so many lakes that ached to be paddled. Alas, the paddleboard got left at home, but I packed up almost everything else.

For Raphael, nearly as much preparation was made: a month's supply of dog food and an assortment of different treats and toys. I even bought a MOLLE vest for him, the sort that K9 dogs wear in the military or police, either in the off chance that he would carry his own water canteen on hikes or because it might just look cool on him. That MOLLE vest was expensive, and I'll admit in advance that we didn't end up using it once. I brought one first aid kit for humans and got another first aid kit specifically for dogs. I brought vitamins and pills and sprays that could come in handy if Hafa had a hot spot or needed to calm down. Everything I could think of to bring, I brought.

October is always a warm month in LA, with an average

high of about 79 degrees, and I was sweating by the time I was halfway through loading up the rig. Along the exterior were numerous large compartments which I utilized as best I could by packing large items that I thought might randomly come in handy, like the skis, the MOLLE vest, packs of bottled water and paper towels. Also, anytime I travel, I always pack some candles to make the places I stay at feel and smell like home, which is something I learned from one of my clients, a brilliant woman who's taught me many things. I also brought a Bluetooth speaker, the mobile hotspot, my camera, my laptop and a box of cigars. I didn't pack any weapons of any kind, assuming that the dog and I could hold off any strangers who might want to cause us harm.

Back in high school I worked at a video rental store and took pride in my own movie collection. This was back when people still bought and rented movies in person. I have a big binder with hundreds of DVDs in it from those days. Given the RV had a television and DVD player, I brought the binder with me to watch movies at night in case the satellite didn't work. The RV's satellite didn't work once during the trip, so that binder ended up being my only option for watching anything.

The RV was fitted with a bathroom and shower, a washer and dryer, an oven, a stovetop and a full-size refrigerator, which I had packed with groceries. I took the majority of my wardrobe into the vehicle too, simply because I could, and I wasn't sure what attire would be needed. I had effectively filled the rig with as many supplies as I could imagine, including six kinds of hot sauce, which I knew my brother would appreciate. In my refrigerator at home, I have at least 20 kinds of hot sauce, so it was a concerted effort to narrow it down to the top six for the drive. Anywhere I travel, I try to buy some local hot sauce.

There are several large windows in my living room that face the ocean and the main street in town, called Hermosa Avenue. Since my couch is near the window, Hafa often lies on the couch and stares at all the people and dogs going by. Brian had told me not to allow Hafa on the couch or bed, but I don't mind and have always allowed both. Hafa watched intently while I packed up the motor home, perched on the couch, perhaps worried that I was moving out and leaving him behind. A few times I stopped and reassured him, patting his head. "Don't worry, big dog; we're going on an adventure. You're coming with me."

The sun set, and I was still slowly packing my things into the rig. I stepped outside the rig onto the sidewalk, and an older neighbor of mine walked up to inspect the vehicle.

"You got room for one more in there?"

"Yeah, hop on in. Next stop is Mexico."

He laughed and told me about a road trip he'd taken years ago and how great a memory it was for him. Then he wished me luck and walked away. I'd been loading and arranging things for hours and was sweaty and tired. I went inside my house and enjoyed one last real shower at home before the drive.

NEVADA

AARON AND HIS WIFE, LAURA, MADE IT TO MY HOUSE earlier than expected, a little after sunset. I gave them a quick tour of my temporary home on wheels and everything I'd packed in it. Aaron brought two small bags and a case of some carbonated juice drink. He'd packed much lighter than I had, but he had some things I hadn't even considered, like hiking boots and a headlamp. A real Boy Scout.

As I showed off the amenities of my temporary home, my brother nodded and professed, "*This* is camping." I laughed and agreed. Laura wished us luck, and then she drove back to their home in San Diego while I poured myself some tea in a thermos and locked the doors to my home for the month. It's some sort of Cordyceps mushroom tea that always keeps me awake late when I drink it.

Then, I finally let Hafa into the RV. He had been anxiously watching me load up the rig all afternoon but was still unclear on whether he'd be joining me. Once inside, Hafa ran around and inspected everything with his booming and powerful nose, then settled onto the couch behind the driver's seat. He was elated that he was going with us and wasn't being left at home.

By 8 p.m. my brother and I were on the road. Sitting way up high and with a giant windshield, it was like driving a spaceship on the road at night. I jumped around from the 405, to the 110, to the 91 and then to the 710 and 105, 605 and 210, just to get from Hermosa Beach to Interstate 15 North, which would then be our path for the foreseeable future. My brother in the passenger seat and Hafa sitting on the floor between us, watching everything out the front windshield, taking it all in.

The bus took wide turns, and we'd gone a ways before I started being able to gauge where I was in the lane based on the side mirrors. But after that, I felt like I was a long-haul trucker and had been on the road my entire life. The steering wheel had a stabilizer which made the driving feel more effortless. Loaded up with a full tank of water, a full tank of gas and a menagerie of supplies, the rig sailed along smoothly. But it burned gas. I was amazed by how quickly it burned gas.

I hadn't prepared any specific playlists for the road trip but figured I'd cobble one together along the journey. Luckily, my brother played DJ for the first few days from his phone to help save me from getting tired of my own tunes too quickly. That night he played plenty of Willie Nelson, John Prine, Bob Dylan and Tom Petty early on, and a lot of Kenny Chesney. His song "American Kids" has a good, upbeat vibe, and I hadn't heard it before, so it became an early theme song for the drive straightaway to amp me up.

The traffic on the highway was light, and I kept it steady at around 60 mph in the right lane. Sometimes a semitruck would pass us and a WHOOSH of air would shoot against the rig, moving us a foot to the right and rattling my nerves. The more I drove the rig, though, the more I got used to how it performed and was able to counter its sways one way or the other like a rhythmic dance.

Aaron and I, having similar sarcastic vibes, would playfully complain with each other. "I wish this RV had a sunroof. And an autopilot feature. It'd be a lot more relaxing if I could just lean back and look up at the stars while the car drove itself like one of those Teslas."

We'd both pretend to be dreadfully upset about each feature we listed that wasn't present. Then one of us would pile on with even more things. "You mean this model doesn't have that, or a Jacuzzi? Ahhh well, I guess that's all right. You already rented it." Then my brother shared a parable. "Have you ever heard the story of the Chinese farmer?"

"No, I don't think so."

"Well, basically, there was a Chinese farmer, and his horse ran away one day. All of his neighbors came by the next day to console him. 'Oh, that's terrible fortune,' they'd tell him. And the farmer would say, 'It could be good; it could be bad.' The next day, his horse returned with seven other wild horses. His neighbors then said, 'What good luck you have. Now you have eight horses!' And the farmer said,

'It could be good; it could be bad.' Then the next day, the farmer's son was trying to break one of the wild horses and fell off and broke his leg. Again, his neighbors chimed in, saying, 'Oh what terrible luck.' And the farmer said, 'It could be good; it could be bad.' Then the next day, the general of the local army came into town to conscript every able-bodied young man into the army, and since his son had a broken leg, he didn't go off to war and die like the rest of the young men in the village."

I told Aaron I liked this story, and we started using the line, "It could be good; it could be bad" for any number of circumstances. Anything I'd complain about or celebrate from then on, he'd say, "It could be good; it could be bad."

We were still a few hours out from Vegas around midnight when I pulled off the highway and parked on the shoulder of the next on-ramp behind a big rig. I was one of them now, so it felt natural to park by them. I assumed the driver of the big rig in front of us was taking a nap or resting, but there was no sign of anyone there. Aaron, Raphael and I all hopped out into the night and took a few moments to marvel at the stars. The sky was clear, and you could see thousands of them in every direction. For the rest of the trip I didn't see a sky so full of stars as I did right there in a ditch somewhere off I-15 North in Nevada that night in early October.

Looking down, the view was less stupendous. There was a sea of trash in this ditch where we'd parked. It was as if someone in every other passing car for five years had tossed something out of their window in order to build up to such an impressive collection of garbage. There were broken glass bottles, dirty used diapers, fast-food wrappers and every other form of trash that people had unburdened themselves of by this highway on their way from LA to Vegas. About 100 yards out in the field was a creepy old wooden shack of some sort that looked like a strong wind might blow it over. No telling what purpose it ever served, but there is no chance it serves any good purposes these days.

"You want to go out there and check out that shack? See what's going on in there?"

My brother had no interest. "Nah. I think this is actually the setting for the next *Saw* movie. Let's get out of here before someone in a mask comes out from behind that tall grass."

We all three relieved ourselves in that creepy, nasty ditch under an extraordinary night sky, then we hopped back into our bus. Aaron offered to drive for a bit, so we switched seats. Both of us were too excited to sleep, and when we stopped for gas we bought some cold coffee drinks to keep us awake for the night. Aaron drove on, and I played some music from the passenger seat. Hafa was tired, so he curled up on the floorboard by my feet, stuck his head under my seat and went to bed.

LAS VEGAS, NEVADA

IT MUST HAVE BEEN AROUND 3 A.M. BY THE TIME WE drove through Las Vegas. The last few times I'd been there had been for decadent and degenerate party excursions, the kind that people flock there to enjoy. One of those times we'd even flown in on one of Cher's private jets, allegedly.

This trip was of a different nature. My brother is sober, and I had assured him that I would stay sober for the five days of the trip when he was there with me, out of solidarity. So we drove past the Vegas strip, late on a Wednesday night. It was good for me to spend a few days sober, in any case. I hadn't been taking terrific care of my health since the breakup, and I really needed a few days of cleansing my system in the fresh air.

At home, I haven't owned a microwave in over ten years. They give me a weird suspicion that they aren't at all healthy, and I get along fine without them. I understand a flame warming something up on a stove or oven or grill, but I don't understand a microwave, so I try to avoid them whenever I can. Since the Southwind had a microwave and I'd brought bags of popcorn, I caved and decided to make some while Aaron drove through town. I turned the generator on and the microwave popped on. I cooked the popcorn, turned the generator off and sat back down, propping my feet up on the dashboard while munching on the tasty and forbidden snack.

There was a strange calm of empty streets that I hadn't seen in Vegas before, bizarre in its serenity. It was late, even for Vegas. The streets were empty, and the people must have all been inside, but the casinos were lit up bright to let us know there was opportunity in there. We kept driving until we were about ten minutes on the outskirts of town and decided to stop for gas again since we didn't know when we'd have another opportunity. Repeatedly, I berated Aaron for not using the turn signal early and often, but in a vehicle that big, people do tend to notice when you're turning, so we survived. A few times I got him to use it, but most often he didn't.

"I've only got a few pet peeves. One of them is people not using their turn signal."

"Oh yeah? Is that right? That's interesting." Aaron didn't really find it interesting or care how many pet peeves I had.

"That girl that I traveled with in Brazil, Monique, told me that she learned how to speak English mostly by watching YouTube videos. Like, other girls that had moved to America had started YouTube channels where they did lessons and gave advice, and she watched those."

Aaron gave a slight nod, with a real lack of interest. "Uh huh."

"And in one of the videos, the lady said, 'If you don't understand something that an American says, just nod and smile or say *interesting*.'"

Aaron laughed. "Interesting."

We got off the highway and rolled into a gas station about 15 minutes east of Las Vegas at 3:30 a.m. We pulled up to a gas pump, and a moment later a lowered Cadillac with tinted windows and shining rims pulled up at the pump across from us. I was exiting my vehicle as the Cadillac driver exited his, and we both admired each other's ride. Hafa is a creature of packs, so when Aaron or I would exit the rig, he'd jump on the dashboard and watch us steadily from the windshield.

The driver of the Cadillac was eyeing the Southwind. "Nice rig you got there."

"Yeah, you too." I realized it sounded stupid as soon as I'd said it, but it didn't matter. He knew what I meant.

"What's that hold, like 100 gallons?"

"I think so, something like that." I had to look up the specifics later to confirm, but he was right. It held both 100 gallons of water and 100 gallons of gas.

"I wish I was driving one of those out on the road right now. You guys have fun."

"Thanks, man, you too." Again, it seemed like a stupid and inappropriate thing to say, but it's easy to give a reflexive "You too."

He went into the gas station. We filled up our tank and climbed back inside the Southwind, and Aaron kept driving us northeast.

By the time the sun came up, we were both exhausted. Aaron was still driving and suggested we find somewhere to park and sleep for a couple hours. Driving through the night sounded great until we'd done it. I looked at one of the apps on my phone and found there was a casino a few miles up the road where we could park. Like most casinos, it had an expansive parking lot surrounding it. When we arrived, there was a separate fenced-in area with numerous RVs, but that seemed like a whole process, and it was early, so we found an empty section of the main lot, took up two spaces and parked off on our own. We didn't level the RV or open the slides. We simply shut off the engine, closed the blinds, crawled into our beds, and passed out.

UTAH

THAT MORNING AS I SLEPT AFTER OUR FIRST STRETCH of driving hundreds of miles in a bus, I had vivid nightmares. I dreamt of daytime scenes, of me driving up curving mountainous roads and then somehow losing control and going over the guardrails, tumbling down to a fiery and explosive death.

Aaron woke me up, and it was still early. I think we only slept for two or three hours. I was miserable and cranky, but Aaron insisted we get moving. He'd made coffee. I complained that the parking lot went on forever and there was no grass for Hafa to use, so we drove around until we found a small patch of grass. We didn't go into the casino, but we appreciated the use of their parking lot nonetheless.

I took the wheel and thought about the nightmare I'd had and that I needed to be extra careful.

BEAVER, UTAH

ONCE WE HAD COFFEE IN OUR SYSTEMS, I WAS DRIVing again, and we went through a small piece of the corner of Arizona and then we were in Utah. By mid-morning we were in Beaver, a city of about 3,000 people. We got off the highway to look for gas and food.

At the intersection, a white van drove by in front of us. It had a huge red flame painted on the side of it. My brother jokingly pointed at it as it drove past us. "Woah. Was that a van or a rocket ship?"

Painting a flame on the side of your vehicle doesn't add anything aesthetically that I'm aware of, but it is a bold statement for a van. I parked at the gas station, and Aaron walked toward a Mexican restaurant for breakfast burritos and more cold coffees. While the gas filled up, I used the squeegee to wash bugs off the windshield from our first night on the road. As I cleaned, a man from the service station and tire shop was clearly scoping out my ride. He walked up in his mechanic gear and pointed at my front right tire.

"Your tread is bare. Did you know that your tread is completely bare?"

It was early and I was still exhausted. I didn't know what he was after. "What's that?"

He directed me to feel the ridges of the tire, then told me to compare that to my other tires. He was right that the others were in much better shape.

"That tire is about to blow; just wanted to warn you. We've got a tire shop right here and I think I have that size in stock." He said it all too casually, like they only had that size of tire there by sheer luck.

Suddenly I was picturing more images of the tire blowing out on the freeway while doing 60 mph and barrel-rolling with more than 20,000 pounds of weight behind me. My brother came back with breakfast burritos and offered me one. I turned him down, as I wasn't hungry enough yet and didn't trust the look of the place. I told him the situation with the tire guy, and then we were both convinced by his fear-mongering sales tactics. So I called OB, the owner of the RV, and he agreed that whatever made us feel safest he would support.

Day two on the road and I was hustled into buying a $500 tire. So the tire was changed, and we were on our way out of Beaver. As we left the parking lot, the tire shop was already changing another tire for a young couple in an RV, and another one of their employees was approaching someone at a gas pump to give them the sales pitch as well. Opening a tire shop and gas station in Beaver, Utah must have been the master plan of some tedious genius, and he should be glad to know that his operation was humming along the way it was that day.

Whether the replacement tire was needed or not, I felt safer as we drove on and left Beaver. So that was comforting at least, if an expensive start to the road trip. "This thing better not need any more parts this month." I committed that I would check the oil regularly, drive her with care and pray for the best. As we pulled out of Beaver, we went over some gravel that shook the motor home so hard that one of the kitchen cabinets swung open. A can of beans fell out and landed *smack* right onto the clay sink cover and shattered it to pieces. I don't even know why an RV needs a cover over the sinks, so I cleaned up the pieces and put them in a closet along with all the other sink covers, and got back on the highway, hoping this thing would hold together for a few more miles without something else breaking.

ZION NATIONAL PARK

ON I-15, ZION IS ABOUT TWO HOURS FROM BEAVER. Closer to three when you're driving a bus, putting us on the outskirts of Zion National Park around midday. It was a Thursday in early October, but the area was still buzzing. As we drove along, we'd see hundreds of cars parked, lots filled to the brim and more cars parked along the side of the road. Making a reservation ahead of time for this first real night actually appeared to be a smart move now, as I was tired and achy and liked knowing we had a specific spot to call our own that night. The only other reservation I'd made was two weeks away, and I was ready to be able to set up camp somewhere other than a casino parking lot surrounded by asphalt and cars.

We went through the south entrance of Zion and paid our fee to go in. We were directed to take our second right to get into South Campground. We checked in there and someone gave us a park map with the rules and info on where our site was and then I pulled around to it. The campground was packed and quite compact, so that sitting by your fire pit you could easily see a number of other campsites in full view. You could be sitting by your own campfire, look around and accidentally catch someone's eye who is sitting by their campfire looking around as well. It was like we were trying to be out in nature, but we were all out there doing it together. Not exactly the secluded isolation I'd been picturing, but it was pretty there at least.

RV campsites seem to me different than tent campsites in terms of their sense of community. People with RVs tend to see it as an entire lifestyle, the way surfing or hunting is a lifestyle. Whenever I was on the road, I would wave to passing RVs, and their drivers would always wave back at me. Throughout my trip, at different sites I would see two or three motor homes parked near each other and a group of people circled around a common campfire. Friends or family would drive alongside each other to different regions to explore and sightsee together. Once you are able to hook up the sewage, water and electricity, you essentially have a tiny home. The campsite in Zion didn't have any hookups, but the feeling was the same. On one hand, I appreciated seeing the camaraderie among these small communities, but on the other hand, I really wanted to have more freedom and space and let Hafa see the world off his leash.

It took me a few minutes to back the rig into our site, my brother standing outside, navigating me between two large Ponderosa pine trees. Eventually we were parked on level ground near the fire pit. I turned on the brakes, leveled the jacks and opened the slides. Suddenly the space inside doubled in size, and we had us a home.

The nature of Zion feels crisp and bright like a photograph: mountains in hues of golden and red. The mountains of rock seem small at a distance, and then your eyes adjust and the mountains start to appear farther and farther away. It's a humbling site, and I now understand why people are drawn there. The campground itself has a lot of trees and shade, but there wasn't a ton of privacy. South Campground is close to many of the popular trails and shuttles, which helps account for why it was so busy there. If we'd been tent camping, we would have had other campground options, with their own pros and cons. Though we were still tired, we went looking for a trail to explore once we'd set up camp. According to Zion's pamphlets, dogs are not allowed on any of their trails except for the kiddie one by the stream, and only while on a leash.

There were also lots of other rules on the pamphlet instructing guests to turn generators off by 8 p.m. and so forth. The result of standardizing best practices for family-friendly camping experiences. Their pamphlet explicitly states that emotional support animals do not qualify as service dogs and that you cannot take them on hikes. I wondered what series of events led to that rule. Perhaps a dog attacked someone, or two dogs fought each other. Maybe a dog fell off a cliff on one of the more dangerous hikes. Whatever their rationale was for the guidelines, we decided to take the dog anyway and show Hafa one of the medium-difficulty hikes. I try to picture a best-case scenario and a worst-case scenario when making decisions, and the worst outcome I could imagine resulting from bringing Hafa on a hike was a park employee telling me to take him back to our campsite. Hafa was part of our group, and I wouldn't go explore without him, so off we went.

As we went up one of the trails, there was a line of people going up and coming back down, all to take photos in the same scenic spots. We had nixed the idea of going to the Grand Canyon before because we assumed there would be throngs of people there and it would be difficult to really enjoy in one rushed day. So here we were at a national park where dogs were ostracized and the trails were completely packed. Don't get me wrong; it's beautiful there. But there are thousands of places in this country with natural beauty, and I don't think people should stand in lines to take identical pictures of them.

About halfway up the trail, we stopped for a water break, and Aaron did some push-ups, though I told him I wasn't impressed at all. Aaron had packed three waters in his bag, and I'd only brought one. I was thirsty and grateful for his forethought. The temperature was in the dry mid-90s, not a cloud in site.

Hafa behaves surprisingly well off leash and stays right by my side for the most part, and I've spent a good deal of time trying to make him reliable off leash. He loves to say hello to people, though, and is just as likely to run up to any other animal he happens to see, since he's still a puppy. On such a busy trail packed with families and couples, I kept him on his leash, and he kept pulling like a maniac that needed to lead the way, like I had never even attempted to leash-train him. He'd see someone and pull his hardest to try and say hello. Even at eight months old, he's a big and intimidating dog to many people, and German shepherds can be intimidating anyway, being associated with aggressive police dogs.

These first few days of the trip were certainly unusual for Hafa and made him act out from being overwhelmed by so many new experiences. He'd pull and I'd try to pull him back, knowing that if only I could let him off leash he'd be so much easier. That didn't seem like an option at all, given how busy this place was and how many rules they had. It was already a faux pas for him to be on the trail at all, let alone off leash. My arms got tired from Hafa pulling his hardest the entire time, and I was agitated by his inability to chill out and listen to me.

"This is nice but will be better once they build a Cheesecake Factory up here." My brother nodded and smiled.

A couple walking down the trail passed us as we were headed up, and Aaron asked them, "Hey, are they still serving tacos up there?" They laughed and kept walking down past us. When Aaron and Laura still lived in Denver, they did a lot of hiking, and when I'd visit them, we'd usually go for a hike in the nearby mountains. Aaron was full of silly things to tell people on the trails. He'd summit a fourteener and on the way down tell people still on their way up, "Hey! Arnold Schwarzenegger is up at the top taking pictures with people and signing autographs. Hurry up." All with a straight face.

We made it to the top and of course we took customary photos of the same scenic views that everyone else did, and then we headed back down to our camp. Along the trail going back down, there was a fork in the path, with the main trail continuing to the left, and something else off to the right. My brother stayed on the main trail, and I veered off to the right with Hafa to check it out. We ended up on some random dirt road, and then we turned back to try and find the main trail. I could see the other trail up the hill a bit, but there were plants and a yellow string roping off our access.

Hafa and I went over the string and walked through the plants to the trail as two middle-aged women with fanny packs were walking by.

"The sign says to stay off the plants, and you're walking right through them, hmmm."

We got to the main trail path and, sure enough, there was a sign on that side of the string saying not to disturb the plants in that area.

"Oh, sorry, we got lost, and there wasn't a sign on that side."

"I don't care, but hope nobody that works here sees you doing that."

The ladies and their fanny packs walked off in a judgmental exuberance, like they'd done their one good deed for the day.

I looked at the sign again, then looked at the plants we'd

walked across to get there. We hadn't done any damage, really, but I was adequately shamed about breaking another of the camp's many rules. Aaron and I wanted to leave our campsites cleaner than we found them, so when I got back to our site, I cleaned up as much trash as I could from the previous tenants to make myself feel honest and partially to make up for my mistake of walking over some sensitive plants on the trail.

Those ladies really got to me about the plants we'd walked over, and I felt like a jerk. Disturbing or ruining habitats was the last thing I wanted to do.

Hafa and I found Aaron and walked back to our site. We cleaned up, made a campfire and cooked some chili-cheese hot dogs. The staple Coney Islander hot dogs in Tulsa that my brother and I both grew up loving.

"Now *this* is camping," my brother kept repeating as we dressed our hot dogs.

I told Aaron how I wanted to be more off the grid and on our own than this. Hafa couldn't even be off leash, making this basically a hotter version of home for him. It was aggravating to me holding the leash with such a strong dog pulling me with his entire strength. I told Aaron that I didn't leave the city to do a Disney-like tour of parks with trails lined with visitors waiting to take the same damned photo in a place that felt like it had even more rules than my Russian neighbor. I wanted to boondock where we could roam freely. I didn't want to see any more rules, fences, fanny packs or roped-off areas of nature.

"Up to you, man. I'm just along for the ride," Aaron would say and shrug.

"Good. Then tomorrow we'll get out of the park and find somewhere off on our own."

"Okay, man; I'm just happy to be out on the road like this. I wish I could come along for more days with you. I'm jealous of all the places you're going to get to see."

Aaron poked around in my DVD collection and picked out *The Departed* as a safe bet. I put on the movie and turned off the lights; we finished our hot dogs and watched the film. I'd forgotten how many great lines are in that movie. It's jam-packed with fantastic dialogue, and we found ourselves quoting along like fanboys. Mark Wahlberg going, "Maybe. Maybe not. Maybe fuck yourself." Such a great movie in every way and easily one of my favorite Scorsese films.

"*This* is camping," Aaron reminded me one more time before he went to sleep on his fold-out couch.

SHEEP BRIDGE ROAD

WE WOKE UP, MADE BREAKFAST AND HAD OUR COFfees. I made bacon and then cooked our eggs in the bacon grease. My brother pointed out that our dad used to make us eggs the same way. Not healthy, but tasty. Since I'd brought several hot sauce options, my brother tried out the Yellowbird sriracha on his eggs and fell in love with it.

"Man, I'm going to put this on everything when I get back home."

After breakfast we went down to the stream by the campground for a bit to let Hafa splash around, with his leash on, of course. Aaron was down to stay for a little longer to explore more of the iconic Zion trails, but I wanted out of this populated mess of fenced-in nature. We drove out of there and went back west a few miles.

Sheep Bridge Road was mentioned in a Bureau of Land Management, or BLM, post I had seen in my research, so we headed in that direction. Any BLM land in the United States will allow you to camp out for free on any single site for 14 days at a time, meaning that if you have the supplies to do so, you can live in one of these rigs and move every 14 days to another site. Many people do this, and bring enough water and propane and groceries to last them for long stretches at a time, living rent-free on public land with a gorgeous view. In Utah alone, there are over 22 million acres of BLM land, so this sort of lifestyle may be more common than you'd imagine.

We went about 9 miles west of Zion to a town called Virgin, Utah. Virgin has a population of 596, and they have a law that requires every homeowner there to have a firearm. A real frontier-justice type place. They've got a small general store called Fort Zion, and the place is set up like an old frontier town, with a fake jail for photos and a petting zoo with llamas. You can buy carrots to feed the llamas and pet them, and they're happy and content as far as llamas go. There was a woman working behind the register that I asked about finding some BLM land. She knew of Sheep Bridge Road and agreed that it was a good option, but she also told us about two other spots that were superb but harder to get to in any vehicle larger than an SUV.

Leaving the general store, the turnoff to Sheep Bridge Road wasn't far. It's a gravel road, so I had to drive slow or else the entire rig would rattle and shake like an earthquake had hit. We went up the length of the road and back to find the most secluded area. It didn't seem like there was another soul for miles. I backed the rig into a spot next to a fire pit, hit the brakes, leveled the jacks and opened the slides. Then we set up the outside area: expanded the awning and laid out our bamboo mat.

On top of the mat, I put the fold-up table and lawn chairs and then put the chessboard, cigars, my laptop, the mobile hotspot and a Bluetooth speaker on the table to make it home. We put on some music, I grabbed a gigantic bone from one of the outer lower compartments where I'd hidden some goodies for Hafa, and put it, along with a few tennis balls and his water bowl, on the bamboo mat, and we'd officially set up camp in record time. I was getting the hang of operating this thing and starting to see why so many people travel this way—now that we were really out on our own.

Before we parked, we had seen an entrance to a trail, so we packed up some waters, locked the RV and went on foot in search of the trailhead. Hafa was off leash and finally starting to grasp his new way of life, and he loved it. He'd run ahead and sniff around and then come back to us and walk alongside me. On a leash he would pull his hardest, but off one he's really like my shadow. What I've heard some people refer to as a Velcro dog. There was a dry heat and more red limestone mountains. We found the trail and followed it for several miles.

"Can you believe this was all underwater at one point?" Aaron asked me. "The plants even look like the kind you'd see in the ocean today, huh?"

It hadn't occurred to me before, but he was right. I could imagine the desert-bound shrubs swaying on the ocean floor. The red clay dirt was spotted for miles with little green shrubs with bright yellow tips packed in dense patches along the trail. Not big enough for a deer to hide in, but you could certainly imagine a snake, or a rabbit, or a lizard hiding away in there.

Aaron works at the San Diego Zoo, and he is always telling me random facts about animals.

"Do you know whether zebras are born white with black stripes, or black with white stripes?"

He knew all manner of factoids you'd learn from working in a zoo. I learned that zebras are black with white stripes, and hippos can run 19 mph.

The sun was beating down hard, and we had to stop several times for water breaks. Hafa's first day exploring off leash, and it didn't seem like he wanted to move to a desert long term. After a few miles, Hafa would go find a patch of shade near one of the big sagebrush shrubs and lie down for a rest, and I would have to keep telling him to "*venha aqui*." The hike we'd done the day before at Zion was new and big for him, and now this trail was even more remote, hotter and drier. He was a tired pup throughout the hike, and we ended up giving him about half our water.

Our trail was also popular for mountain bikers, as we saw two riding by fast and furious. Otherwise we didn't see anyone else for several miles. Eventually the trail led us to Hurricane Cliffs.

"Hurricane, Utah. Must be named after a big hurricane that came through here," my brother joked, and I laughed.

On the ridge of the cliffs, you can see a giant canyon that goes on for miles and miles. It's an awesome site, and I'm sure it would be a great but terrifying spot to go mountain biking along its ridge like that. There is a vista at the midway point of the hike overlooking Hurricane Cliffs, and along the railing there is a placard for the men who determined to build the Hurricane Canal. A 7.5-mile canal built entirely by hand and completed in 1904. Here we were 115 years later, and I couldn't conceive of building anything by hand out there. Somehow, James Jepson and John Steele decided in 1893 that they needed to do this, and they made it happen.

"I can't believe they were out here carving a 12-foot bed for a canal into limestone with hand tools. What the hell was this John Steele guy thinking?"

"Them guys were tough. There used to be men of conviction and great ideas in this world. Now most people are lazy. When was the last time you heard of someone with a big idea?"

After my brother said this, we both looked at each other, nodded in agreement, then looked back down over the cliffs for a moment before heading back toward the camp.

Walking back on the trail, Aaron taught me some strange facts about LED lights that I still don't understand. Once we got to our campsite, Hafa drank some more water and then collapsed in the shade on our bamboo mat under the awning and went right to sleep. My brother hadn't played chess before, so I taught him and then we played several games. He quickly got the hang of it, and we played over and over until our brains were tired, and then he went to start the fire.

I cooked us some steaks, and Aaron made campfire potatoes the way our dad would back when we'd gone camping with him. He'd peel and chop the potatoes, then toss them into aluminum foil with some butter, chopped onions, garlic and seasonings, then fold the foil up and put the whole thing in the campfire. We had cigars and sat by the fire watching a beautiful sunset over the desert landscape. The steaks were great, the potatoes were great and we were all tired. Two days of exploring the desert and my body was burnt and dehydrated, and my dog slept and slept like he was in a coma.

After dinner, Aaron picked out *The Big Lebowski* from my DVD collection, and we put it on. It's possible I've seen that movie over 200 times, but it still never gets old.

"*This* is camping," I told him.

"Yeah, man, this *is* camping."

The next morning we had our breakfast and coffees, I had a cigar, and we played a few more games of chess while Hafa ran around on his own. He'd disappear off into the distance, and after a while I'd call and whistle for him to come back. Hafa would run back to us at full speed, tongue hanging out of his mouth, happy as a clam. It was Saturday, and we were lazy for a few hours. I knew that the next day would be busier, though, as Sunday would be the sixth: Aaron's birthday and the day he'd need to catch his flight from Salt Lake City. Everything felt right at Sheep Bridge Road, being unplugged and off the grid with my brother, and I already didn't want him to leave. We'd started the first few days of the journey right and were just settling into a good groove.

Aaron wasn't helpful at all in deciding our last day's itinerary. "I'm just along for the ride," he'd say when posed with any question of substance.

"Yeah, but it's your birthday tomorrow; where should we go? What should we do?"

"I'm having a good time, man; it's up to you."

We would go in a circle like this a few times, so I decided we'd head north and stay the night somewhere before Provo. Then we could wake up the next day, go to Provo and spend some time with our sister and our nephew and his wife before continuing on to Salt Lake City. I'd booked Aaron a midnight flight, and first class usually gets you through the security line pretty quickly, so I figured we could set up camp in SLC and have dinner, then order him an Uber to the airport.

I looked up a campsite in SLC, then typed in that location and the airport on Uber to make sure it was doable, and it told me a driver could be there in 20 minutes and the ride would be $40 or so. I was confident that Sunday's schedule was achievable, so we just needed to find a place to stay for the night between Virgin and Provo.

"You know, you don't have to pay for the Uber to the airport tomorrow. I can call it from my phone."

My brother wanted to pitch in for the trip more, but I was grateful that he had even joined the maiden voyage, and I wanted to handle it all for his birthday.

"No, I've got it. Plus, I have Uber Diamond, so it should prioritize getting us a driver to come out all that way, maybe."

"Strange flex, but okay. Thanks, man."

SOMEWHERE IN UTAH

WE KNEW THAT WE'D FIGURE OUT A PLAN ALONG the way, so we got back on the road and left Virgin for good. I can't remember where we got off the highway, but there was some small town, so we stopped and bought some groceries. The grocery store was quaint, and all its beef options had expired the week before. The girl working the register must have been in high school. She probably had no idea about the expired meat. I asked her if she knew of any campgrounds nearby. She shrugged and shook her head. Helpless.

I bought some ChapStick, as Utah's dry air had made my lips red and swollen. The ChapStick soothed my sore lips, and we drove around the little town. We happened to pass a KOA RV campground, and it sounded reasonable to have water and electric hookups for the night and stop there.

When we got to the campground it was nearly full. There were a few empty spots near a fence overlooking a field, so I requested the corner spot, and we had at least a small area to ourselves. Aaron went and used the campground shower, and I tried out the shower inside the rig. It was my first time using it, and I didn't turn on the propane and the water heater first, so the shower was a cold, weak stream. Aaron came back looking fresh and told me the showers inside were clean and felt great.

Since we were back in a crowded campground, I took out a 30-foot leash I'd brought, tied it to a picnic table and hooked Hafa to the other end. Not quite like being off leash, but it was another nice day with a delightful sunset and fresh air. I'd brought some nylon strings for the guitar, and I convinced Aaron to restring and tune the guitar for me, then he played us a few songs.

I cooked us some dinner and put on the movie *High Plains Drifter*, with Clint Eastwood as a man's man playing the Stranger: "The only problem you've got, Sheriff, is a short supply of guts." The days had been long, the sun had been powerful and we were tired, so we both fell asleep before the movie had ended.

PROVO, UTAH

AARON HAD WOKEN UP EARLY AND GONE FOR A RUN, and then he had been chased by some mean dog and gotten away by jumping a fence. Started his birthday off with cool air and a heart-pumping race from a vicious dog. I opted for a real shower inside the offices that morning, and for the first time in days I felt clean and refreshed. I had brought my backpack to the showers with a change of clothes and some toiletries but hadn't remembered to bring a towel, so after my shower I found myself drying off with my dirty clothes and then changing into my clean clothes.

Aaron played us some guitar at the picnic table while I had my coffee. He played John Prine's "Angel From Montgomery" and we both sang along. After a few songs we were ready to go, and in no time, I was bringing in the slides, retracting the jacks, turning off the brakes, and pulling back out onto the road.

I'd suggested we meet our nephew, his wife, and our sister somewhere for lunch in Provo since they were all there, but my nephew sent us his address instead and insisted we stop by their house. So we rolled into Provo and parked at a nearby hospital and jumped out. The city seemed clean. Otherwise, since it was a Sunday and all their businesses are closed on Sundays, the streets were fairly empty and life seemed quiet.

Our nephew, Blake, and his wife, Taylor, are Mormon. My sister Angela is not, but it seems like she's been embracing it and learning more about the religion. It was the weekend of the Mormons' October General Conference, which is one of two big conferences the church puts on each year. My sister had come out from Tulsa for the weekend to visit, and they'd been watching the conference on television all weekend, so it was a coincidence that we were able to see her as well.

Blake and Taylor lived in a two-story apartment complex, in a two bedroom on the second floor. Inside, it resembled most two-bedroom apartments I had seen, but they had cute pictures of the two of them everywhere and Christmas lights hanging on the walls to enliven the atmosphere. Blake offered us some pizza rolls he'd just pulled out of the oven. I didn't eat any, but he had a ridiculous mound of them on a platter. There must have been 80 pizza rolls, there were so many. We thought it was funny, but Blake is always smiling and has such a warm spirit that we laughed and asked all about their lives in Utah and their plans in China.

I sat on the floor of the living room with Hafa next to me, still on his leash. My brother sat in one chair while Blake and Taylor sat on the couch across from him. My sister, Angela, sat on the floor as well and kept looking around like she was happy that we were all together again. Angela has always worn her heart on her sleeve. Then she'd say, "Isn't it great that we're all here together?" Blake must get his eternal optimism from her.

Blake and Taylor talked about how they planned to move to China to teach English and start their own business there. Blake had done his two-year mission there and had already learned Mandarin. Taylor had traveled a lot, too, but she hadn't been to China before. They seemed fit for the challenge, though, and I admired them for jumping into new territory to take a risk like that. After a while, Blake pulled out his iPad.

"Do y'all mind if I record you guys telling stories about Papa? It's so rare to have you all in the same place."

"I'll pass."

I said this quickly, and it would have made the ambiance awkward if the audience hadn't included my brother and sister, who know I am likely to say something like this.

The idea of recording us telling stories about my father for some sort of YouTube documenting purpose felt contrived, though I knew my nephew had the best intentions. He admired and respected his grandfather in a way that too few people do. I was simply not prepared mentally or emotionally to go down that road.

"Yeah, I'll tell some stories for you," my brother offered to not be a jerk.

Aaron and Angela told a few stories for him on camera while I took Hafa for a walk around the block. When I got back, we told a few more stories about our dad, Jimmy, off camera and laughed and smiled and then said our goodbyes. Aaron, Hafa and I hugged them all and left in search of food that wasn't pizza rolls, but seriously, every place was closed because it was Sunday. We stopped at a grocery store that was open, bought some potatoes and salmon and drove on to Salt Lake City.

INTRO TO TRAVEL

I MUST HAVE BEEN 8 YEARS OLD OR SO WHEN MY brother went to Key West with my dad for a boys' trip. I remember seeing a picture of them and feeling shafted. My big brother with his snow-white hair must have been around 11 or 12, smiling big with missing teeth and a Hawaiian shirt, standing next to our dad, who was wearing a striped polo tucked into shorts, with parted hair and a powerful mustache. They were in front of a big, colorful striped buoy by the pier that was there simply for touristy photos like this. It said things on each stripe, such as "The Conch Republic," "90 Miles to Cuba," "The Southernmost Point" and "Continental USA." When I saw the photo, I immediately asked why I didn't get to go somewhere like this with my dad. I certainly didn't say, "Awesome, how was the trip?"

Though I hardly remember them being gone, I definitely remember them getting back and seeing that photo. When I then asked why I didn't get one of these cool dad trips along with a commemorative photo, my mom and dad basically agreed with me and told me that I could pick anywhere in the United States to go for a few days with my dad. That's how I remember it all, at least. We weren't rich, but it was summer and my mom was able to get us standby tickets through her job working with an airline. Plus, it seemed like my parents had either already decided that I'd get a trip with my dad beforehand or they weren't surprised by the request, because it all seemed to happen seamlessly.

Perhaps they were always fair like this, or it was possible they knew it was an easy solution to keep me from whining. This was all before my parents divorced, so maybe they just needed some time apart. However it was decided, I excitedly went into my room and spent some serious time studying a small laminated map of North America that I had in my school supplies. When I emerged from my room, I pointed out the northeast of North America on my map to them and announced that I had decided on Washington, D.C. as the one place I really wanted to go see with my dad, and so it was decided. D.C. would be my Key West.

I remember a lot from that D.C. trip with my dad and how cool it was to be out on the road and in a big, important city, just the two of us. I remember us both being happy, and the weather was a clear, bright summer backdrop. He took me to the museums and monuments, and we went to Arlington, Virginia and to the eternal flame at JFK's tombstone. The Museum of American History at the Smithsonian was one of my favorite parts of the trip. It was as though we were both in awe most of the time, pointing at different specimens like two kids.

My parents took all of us kids on a number of trips during my childhood. My dad got a motor home at one point, and we'd all go camping in it sometimes, at places like Robbers Cave State Park. Robbers Cave is a legendary area where outlaws from days past would hide out from the law. People like Jesse James and the Dalton Gang. My dad loved those kinds of stories and would tell us about them when we were camping. After my parents divorced, they'd take us on separate trips, and my dad took my brother and me skiing up in Colorado a number of times. Looking back, I know I had no reason to be entitled to a trip to D.C., and I also know that my parents didn't mean to spoil me. But they did encourage our interests and said yes about D.C., and I love that. They encouraged saying yes and going.

On one of the last days of the trip, we saw a hot dog vendor on the sidewalk, and we both wanted one. As I was handed my hot dog, I put a few things down on the top of a newspaper dispenser, including the disposable camera I had been using to document our trip. The hot dog was a mediocre street dog, and after eating it, I completely forgot the disposable camera and left it on top of the newspaper stand. After 15 minutes or so, we remembered it and traced our steps back to the right newspaper stand next to the right hot dog vendor, but the camera was gone. Not having any pictures of that trip was disappointing, but I still have the memories and tons of gratitude to my parents for encouraging adventure and saying yes.

Traveling alone can be unique and rewarding, but traveling with someone and sharing the experience has often been more memorable and more rewarding to me. And if it isn't on camera, it's still quite good. Maybe even better. Like Heisenberg's uncertainty principle, I believe you can affect something merely by watching it or documenting it. Living without posing for cameras always makes the moment more meaningful. The experience together wasn't about the likes or being seen; it was about us adventuring together and living in the moment.

When my father was diagnosed with lung cancer about ten years later, I was 18. I could have sat with him then to record interviews firsthand and had some stories memorialized with his classic charm and smile. I had a camera throughout high school, and I was obsessed with filmmaking and often recorded things and made short films. Instead, I convinced myself that it was better to enjoy my time with my dad without the distractions of cameras and the inevitable posturing it would bring. No matter what you decide to leave in the frame and include in the edit, you're leaving out giant chunks of authenticity.

That's what I told myself, at least. It's a regret for me now that if I have kids they won't have as much footage of their grandfather as they could have had. Today it is much more common for people to have a podcast or do a masterclass and document their philosophies to pass them down to others. And I think it's great now in many ways. As much as I loved my father, the idea of needing something on camera struck me as arbitrary in comparison to getting to spend more time really together.

My dad, Jimmy, was raised as a Jehovah's Witness, and they don't celebrate holidays. Something about that always struck me, in that there aren't specific days that are good or meaningful. Every day can be meaningful. This is probably where I gained my admiration for that Osho quote, "I live my life based on two principles. One, I live as if today was my last day on earth. Two, I live today as if I am going to live forever."

A memory may be meant to be something for a man to keep candidly to himself, and the decisions we made in the past cannot be changed. So now I'm stuck with my belief, right or wrong, that a moment is best without a camera and without an audience and that every day can be great or meaningful if you embrace it.

SALT LAKE CITY, UTAH

"THAT KID'S GOT A GOOD HEAD ON HIS SHOULDERS."

I was talking about my nephew as we pulled out of the hospital parking lot in Provo.

"Yeah, he's going to be just fine," my brother agreed, and that's all that needed to be said.

Still, it is more than can be said for many people. I have no doubt you could drop my nephew Blake somewhere in China and he'd be on his feet within a few days. With a good partner in Taylor, I was sure he'd be fine wherever he ended up. He's an optimist with a great work ethic, which is a winning combination as far as I know.

We drove north. The big Mormon convention was in town and promised to make the traffic worse, so we dodged downtown and went to the outskirts of the city to East Canyon State Park, which is a good 40 minutes or so east of Salt Lake City. As we drove up and down mountains to get there, we both started feeling a little more skeptical about the likelihood of an Uber actually coming out all that way. And how sketchy the situation would seem for that driver: two guys out in the middle of nowhere that need a ride for some reason. All we needed was an ax to make us seem like bad movie villains.

We got to the park, and in the entire place there was only one other RV. It may have been empty because it was October, or because it was Sunday, or because most people were watching their big Mormon conference. Either way, we had the place to ourselves, and it felt great.

We grabbed a spot and took Hafa off leash to go check out the lake. As the sun went down it began getting cold, so we made a fire and I started cooking dinner. I grilled the salmon and made mashed potatoes with blue cheese in them. Aaron said it was the finest meal I had made on the entire trip, and I think he was right. I'd gotten to spend a few days camping with my big brother, including his birthday, and I knew the RV would feel silent and lonely once he'd gone. Like Blake, my brother has an upbeat warmth to him that makes everyone feel at ease.

After we ate, I decided to go ahead and call the Uber, but it took me 15 minutes to find cell reception, and every time I requested a ride it would either time out or the drivers simply wouldn't accept the ride. I tried this on another rideshare app, and then another. None of the three would work, and my reception kept going from one bar of service to none. For a moment I was concerned he could possibly miss his flight, but my brother and I are problem solvers, so we stayed positive and neither of us showed any signs of panic. Eventually I gave in and decided to look up the taxi service nearby and simply called one to come out there and then go back to the airport.

It took some convincing still, including a ridiculous fare and a sizable tip, but the taxi was ordered and arrived about an hour later. We turned on the Southwind's fog lights when the taxi entered the campground so it'd know where we were parked. I imagine the driver would have been unnerved, for the reasons mentioned previously. In any case, we said our goodbyes and had a hug, and then my brother was gone. Aaron made it to the airport right in time to board his plane and take off. One hour he was sitting by a campfire with only a handful of people within 10 miles, and then literally the next hour he was on a plane heading back to San Diego, smelling like a campfire. He left his hiking boots and headlamp for me to use on the rest of the trip, and both were crucial.

After Aaron left, I went back into the rig and found that Hafa had conveniently knocked my mobile hotspot into his water bowl, rendering it useless. Being able to connect to the internet and work remotely was key to my plan, and just like that, Hafa let it be known that he didn't care about my plans one bit. I pulled a bottle of whiskey out of a bag I had hidden away and poured myself a glass. The first sip of alcohol I'd had in over five days. I took Hafa out and stood by the dwindling fire, had a cigar and my whiskey and suddenly felt truly alone. Hafa sniffed around looking for signs of Aaron. The dog pack had been altered, and Aaron's absence was obvious to us both.

Once we were tired enough and the fire was sad enough, we went back inside. I knew that while running the generator I could plug in the two portable electric heaters I had, but I hadn't realized how simple it was to use the propane heating system in the rig yet. When I turned off the generator, the two portable electric heaters were still plugged in, and that blew a fuse, which made the power inverter stop working, so I had no TV and no heater running.

"All right then."

I turned to Hafa and shrugged, defeated. He cocked his head and looked at me, like he was trying to figure out what I meant by that. It all seemed beyond my ability to solve for the night. I was proud to have even gotten Aaron his taxi in time, so I read a few chapters of a book and went to sleep, drunk from the altitude and from drinking for the first time in a week.

The next morning when I woke up, it was freezing. I was cold and Hafa was colder. I opened my eyes and Hafa was lying on top of me, curled up tight and completely covering my torso, his head shivering into my shoulder. I put my arms around him and rubbed his belly, and he gave me a sad, shivering look, like "Take me back to the hot desert, please."

I'd never seen him so cold, so I took him outside to run around and try to warm up. I don't know how cold it was, but I could see my breath. I tossed a tennis ball a few times and got him running around. Gradually, as the sun came out, the temperature was comfortable again. I went to turn on the generator, but it wouldn't start. I had no cellphone reception so I couldn't call OB, and of course I had no Wi-Fi. Without any coffee or breakfast, I started the rig, brought in the slides, pulled up the jacks, turned off the brakes and got back on the road. It was Monday morning, I was cold and I wanted to see Wyoming.

WYOMING

I FIGURED I WOULD TRY MAKING IT TO JACKSON THAT day. Like most days of the trip, I didn't have a specific agenda or a place chosen to stay at. I'd never been to Jackson, and it just sounded nice. I took the 80 East to the 89 North and wove across the Idaho-Wyoming border for several hours. I called OB, and he explained how to use the propane heater and made a few suggestions for getting the generator to start. Higher altitude and colder weather both supposedly make the generator finicky, though. I pulled over and tested his system and got the generator to start. Voila! Things were going my way.

As I drove, Hafa sat next to me and began licking my arm, then he'd give my elbow a nudge with his nose, then rest his whole head on my knee. I wasn't sure why he was doing this, but a few miles later I pulled over and let him out and he ran to the nearest grass to relieve himself. He really needed to go, and I apologized for driving and driving and not thinking of him. Now I knew that if he licked my arm and nudged my elbow again, it meant he wanted out.

I stopped in Afton, Wyoming, finally feeling tired, and got some gas. Every man in that part of the country wears a hat, so I pulled out a hat I'd brought and popped it on my head. At home in LA I have never worn hats, but I wanted to blend in. Mine was a tan trucker hat with a red bill that said "Pettijohn Construction" across the top. One of the hats my dad had made for his company when I was in high school, and for the foreseeable future I'd be wearing it. There was a cowboy-looking bar next to the gas station, so after I gassed up, I went over for a burger and a beer.

The place was empty, and the burger was okay. There was a pool table, and I could imagine it getting fun in there at night, but I was the only customer that early. I finished my beer, ate half of the burger, paid and left.

ALPINE, WYOMING

DRIVING ON THE HIGHWAYS IN WYOMING FEELS THE same as driving on the highways in California and Nevada and Utah. There are rest stops along the way, gas stations and Subway restaurants. There were more and more billboards warning about opiate addiction and fewer billboards about prayer than there were in Utah. The days of quaint mom-and-pop diners and regional accents and customs have largely been replaced in this country over the decades with fast-food chains and brand names, so the main differences found from one town to another are the terrain and the weather.

Driving on the interstate in a big rig takes a toll on your posture, and hours of driving each day was making me more sore and achy than usual. How some are able to do this full time, I have no idea. Cars and semis fly by as you keep steady in the right lane, taking in as much of the scenery as you can at such a speed. I wasn't too far away from Jackson, but I wanted to park, have a drink and relax, so instead I stopped in Alpine just because it was there. On the way into town I looked up a spot, a park called Greys River Cove, on an app and called them to make a reservation before I arrived. The man told me there'd be an open space waiting for me.

When I pulled up to the RV park, I went in through the side entrance and drove around to a small building where a man was sitting on a folding chair and watching TV. I got out of the rig and approached him.

"Hey there. I called earlier about a spot for tonight."

"Yeah, I told you to turn in at the entrance by the bar. You aren't supposed to use the entrance over there. It's not even usually open; we had to tow the rooster over here today, though."

A cantankerous old coot if I ever met one. I looked over to see the giant sculpted rooster he was talking about.

"That's a nice rooster."

The man got up and came outside of his shack, and he must have been 6-foot-7 and 300 pounds. He was a burly guy with gray hair and a beard that made him look like an aging Paul Bunyan.

"Maybe someone else called you too, and you told them about where to pull in. I remember our whole conversation, and you did not tell me where to pull in. I'm here now, though, and just need to book the spot for one night."

I couldn't seem to drop my big-city sense of entitlement and said it all like a true asshole.

The guy seemed confused, like he had only wanted an apology. But I was tired, thirsty and grumpy.

"Come on in."

He waved me into his little shack as he sat back down and shuffled around for the paperwork. He'd told me the price was $65 on the phone. I remembered the whole conversation clearly.

"How much did I say the space was for one night?"

"You said $55."

"Right, okay. Fifty-five." He started filling out some paperwork. There were obviously no standard rates here. "I'll need your credit card. The machine is inside."

"Oh, well then I'll come inside with you. I don't like to let my card out of my sight."

He looked at me like I was trying to give him shit now.

"Look, I'm not going to steal your credit card."

"Nothing personal. I'll just come inside with you."

He grunted, and I followed him inside. There was a saloon full of young men drinking beers, probably locals. He ran the credit card, I signed the receipt and we walked back outside together as he pointed me toward the direction of my spot.

"You're in site 28; pull in forward, then you'll back out that way and leave in the morning over here by the rooster, where you were supposed to come in. Here's your receipt with the code for the bathroom and the Wi-Fi."

Our space was next to a fence that overlooked a huge preserve with mountains and fields and a portion of Snake River.

"Is there any place I can take my dog to run around?"

"Well, yeah, you can play fetch over here. Just try to clean up after him."

"What about across the fence? Is that public property?"

"Yeah, that's public; you can take the dog off leash over there all you want."

It was the kind of thing I'd been waiting to hear for days. Some country land where the dog wasn't shunned. I shook the man's hand and moved the rig over to our space and parked. I'd brought a bunch of disposable coffee cups, so I poured a beer into one and took Hafa across the fence. He started out a bit apprehensive of his boundaries, sniffing around here or there but staying close. He dipped his toes in the river, then ran back to me. Then I waved my hands in the air, "Go play," and he took off into some tall grass and was gone.

Hafa was running full speed in one direction, then in another, occasionally looking back at me to make sure this was all approved behavior. Doing zoomies in figure eights. He ran down to the water and splashed around, then back up to me as if to say, "Can you believe this?" Hafa ran his heart out like he'd been waiting to be there his entire life. I could tell he was starting to understand why we'd spent so much time driving. We'd arrived, and it was the kind of day that dogs dream about.

I took my phone out to record videos of him running in circles in complete bliss. At eight months old, he'd been raised in an overpoliced city of leashes and fences and rules. And here there were seemingly no rules and few people. That was the best day Hafa had ever had up until then. Once it got dark out, he was tired and we went back to the RV. I went about setting up camp. I set the brakes, leveled the jacks and opened the slides. I hooked the rig up to electricity and water and then decided it was time I try out emptying the sewage tanks.

There were two old white-haired white men with their wives in the two RVs next to me, and both of the men helped show me how to properly do the hookups and empty the tanks. They both had bigger, newer, fancier rigs than I had. It seemed like they knew what they were doing, and I kept thanking them for the help.

It seemed to me that a lot of the other RVs I noticed were being driven by old white men, and they were usually accompanied by their wives. I didn't see many people my age, or many single women out driving motor homes by themselves, and I saw few people of color. This may have been anecdotal, though, since OB, who I had rented the Southwind from, was African-American himself. I'm sure there are statistics on this somewhere, but I'll assume that my experience was representative, as people do.

"How much of the time do you and your wife go on the road like this?" I asked the shorter of the two old white men.

"We spend about half the year on the road. The other half at our home."

"Wow, that sounds amazing. Where are y'all coming from?"

"We were just up in Yellowstone yesterday. We'll stay here for a few days to figure out where's next. What about you? Where are you heading?"

"I was planning on going north in the morning. Yellowstone too."

"Well you're parked facing north. That's what I try to do, too, ha ha, just wake up and start driving in whatever direction I'm facing. There's a storm coming in up there; it was chasing us all the way down."

I'd been on the road for several days and just then realized I hadn't checked a weather forecast once. Living in LA will do that to you, since the weather never changes there. I also hadn't listened to the news or checked in on reality once on the trip. I thanked the two old men again for their help, climbed inside the rig and looked at my maps for a possible destination for the next day.

I told Hafa, "Maybe if we get far enough north tomorrow, we can beat the storm and make it to Bozeman early."

The sun went down, and it rained for the rest of the night. I fed Hafa and walked him again, then locked him in the RV and decided to check out one of the bars down the street. It was still raining, so I jogged over to the Bull Moose Lodge and Saloon. The bar had a log cabin kind of atmosphere and there were only a few people inside when I got there. I sat at the bar and breathed a little easier. I ordered a beer, a bowl of chili and a side of jalapeño poppers.

The place filled up with some more regulars but still wasn't busy or bustling by any means. A group of younger folks was at the pool table, and a few random men were at the bar. Eventually all the seats around the bar were full. On my left was a burly, bearded man of maybe 40, and on my right was an older man in his mid-70s dressed in a cowboy hat, cowboy boots and jacket. The man on my left was quiet; he ordered his beer and then didn't say another word. He sat there drinking stoically, but the old cowboy started talking to me, and then hardly ever stopped. I told him that I hadn't planned on stopping in Alpine, that it sort of happened by chance.

"Oh yeah, that's what happened to me too," he said. "I was heading somewhere else and I ended up in Alpine; that was 30 years ago, and I've never left. This is the best damn town in the world, I'll tell ya."

He went on about his life and the different jobs he'd had. Apparently he knew everyone else at the bar.

"That guy sitting next to you is a real good friend of mine. His name is Mad Dog. Hey Mad Dog."

The quiet guy on my left looked up at his name and said hello to the old cowboy. I introduced myself to them both. Then Mad Dog went back off to his silent state, and I kept talking to the old cowboy.

"So why do they call him Mad Dog?"

"Because he acts like a mad dog."

The cowboy seemed to think this was self-explanatory. Mad Dog nodded in agreement.

My food arrived, and I was hungry. Mad Dog and the old cowboy kept catching up, and more people streamed into the bar, but I focused on my food. The chili was perfect after a long drive and a cold, rainy night, and the jalapeño poppers tasted better than any I've had elsewhere. Most places buy frozen ones and toss them in the fryer, but these tasted freshly made. If not, I must have been really hungry, because they were great. This was my comfort food, and I insisted Mad Dog try one of the jalapeño poppers.

After I ate, I left my drink at the bar to go out and smoke a cigar. When I went out front, there were several people smoking outside on the front porch with drinks in hand. I'd forgotten that in some parts of this country you can still bring your drink outside with you. A real relaxed freedom that had been sucked out of places like LA. I practically ran back inside to grab my drink, then found a rocking chair on the front porch to enjoy a post-dinner cigar and the rain. There was a girl around my age smoking a cigarette and sitting in the rocking chair next to me. We talked about different things I should see or do in Wyoming and Montana. I told her I was headed to Yellowstone next.

"You think we'll see any bears up there?" I asked her.

"Oh, I saw a bear yesterday, right over there on main street. I filmed it on my phone."

She took her phone out and pulled up a video from the day before, shot from the inside of a car looking out the windshield. Sure enough, the video showed a bear standing up straight in an intersection there in Alpine. It was standing there looking around, not caring about any traffic delays it was causing.

Her friend came out to grab her, and they went back inside the bar. The old cowboy and Mad Dog both came outside and talked to some of their friends for a while, and Mad Dog wasn't quiet anymore. It was like he'd needed a certain amount of beer before he could begin having conversations with anyone. Now he was telling jokes and showing his personality.

The rest of the guys on the front porch were all friends who'd driven into town that week from Southern California. They were all in their mid-20s to early 30s. One of them was a contractor doing some work in Alpine and had brought in the rest of these guys to help with a job.

"There's a lot of work up here and you can get 25 bucks an hour," a skinny guy with long hair told me excitedly.

We talked about what towns in Southern California we were from and different places we frequented there. The same bars we knew and so forth. As it was getting later, everyone was getting drunker and sloppier. The skinny guy with long hair was as drunk as anyone, and when I told him about how I was driving around in an RV with my dog, he got really excited.

"Man, that's something I've always wanted to do. I wish I could do that! Where all are you going?"

"Well, I've got a rough idea here on this app." I showed him the app on my phone that had a map with my basic itinerary on it, going up to Montana and then back west and in a loop back down home to California.

"Cool, man. I've never been to Montana. You know

where you should go, if you're doing a road trip?" He'd seen my map, so he knew the general area I was covering.

"Where should I go?"

"Kentucky. It's so beautiful, man, I grew up there."

Had he really looked at the map? I had a small circle around the Pacific Northwest. The east coast wasn't a part of my plan. In fact, I only had about eleven states I'd be driving through over the next few weeks, none of them anywhere near Kentucky; it would be impossible. This guy was not getting it.

"Yeah, I'd love to see Kentucky sometime. Won't work on this trip, but maybe next time. Wendell Berry is one of my favorite writers; he's a Kentucky guy."

The skinny guy with long hair nodded and gave a drunk smile. I went back inside and had another drink. The bar was emptying and there were only two people still inside other than the bartender and me. There was one guy who was slurring and telling me "how fucking hammered" he was planning to get that night. He kept on. "I'm getting fucking hammered tonight." The other guy was ignoring the commotion, standing off in a corner.

"That's good, man, good luck."

"Hey, that's a nice jacket. Is that a Carhartt or Levi? Man, I'm going to get absolutely plastered tonight."

There was one other guy with the out-of-town construction crew still outside the bar who seemed to be on some sort of speed and was starting some shit with Mad Dog for some reason. I didn't want to stick around to find out what Mad Dog would do to the guy, and I'd had enough, so I closed my tab, walked back to my rig and went to sleep.

YELLOWSTONE NATIONAL PARK

THE NEXT MORNING I TOOK HAFA AND MY COFFEE across the fence and spent some time playing fetch and relaxing by Snake River. Despite being in an RV park packed in next to other rigs like sardines, we were steps away from this open land where we could do as we pleased, and I had learned how to empty the sewage tanks. I wanted to get to Yellowstone before the weather turned. I only needed to do 149 miles up US-89 North. At this point that sounded like an easy day. When I pulled out of the RV park, I exited by the rooster like the guy had told me to, since that was so damned important, and I promised Hafa that we'd go back there again someday since he liked it so much. He really loved that place, and I agreed with the old cowboy that there was something special about Alpine.

I drove through Jackson but didn't honestly take it all in since I didn't stop. From a glance, it seemed like a slightly less pretentious version of Aspen that would probably be fun to travel to and ski with someone and stay at a hotel or something. I was with a dog and on a bus, so I drove through and stopped on the highway a few times to walk Hafa and take some pictures of the mountains of Grand Teton National Park. Wyoming is a free and magnificent place, and Hafa agreed. *This* was camping.

Somewhere along the road I noticed a few signs for fireworks sales. Like the skis and guitar I had brought, I figured it'd be better to have fireworks and not need them than to need fireworks and not have them. I exited the highway, and there were two fireworks stores directly across the street from each other. Both big enough to be grocery stores. I chose one, got a shopping cart and loaded up. They had all sorts of "buy one, get one free" type of deals, so I got a few big-daddy fireworks displays and put them in one of the storage bins in the outside of the RV.

I got back on the road and made a few phone calls.

Yellowstone National Park takes up a huge area of land that you could spend a week exploring. So, like in Zion, I knew that I wouldn't get to completely experience or appreciate it all, especially with a dog and strict park rules about being on leash. As soon as you drive into the park you lose all cellphone reception, so I just followed signs toward Old Faithful, and Hafa and I enjoyed the scenery outside the windows. Hafa sat in the passenger seat and stared out the windows, occasionally looking back over at me to make sure I was seeing this same lush forest that he was seeing. Occasionally I would reassure him with an, "I know, buddy."

The road winds around and the speed limit is slow, and I had to stop in a row of cars at one point waiting for a small herd of buffalo to cross the road. I was feeling anxious about not having cellphone service for any amount of time at all. *What if a client needs me? What if something urgent happens?* We make ourselves think we're so important that we must be immediately reachable. I was anxious, and hungry, and practically out of gas. And my phone was worthless.

Luckily, about halfway through Yellowstone there was a small gas station and convenience store. I filled up with gas and asked the two men working there if there was any place with Wi-Fi within striking distance. They directed me to one of the nearby hotels, the only one still open for the season. Old Faithful was nearby, so I went over and took a look, then went to the hotel lobby to find some precious internet so I could start looking up a place for us to stay for the night. I picked out Madison Campground and made a reservation.

Madison Campground is inside of the park, so it didn't take me long to get there. Once I arrived, I was greeted by the park employees to check in. All of the employees were super friendly, kind folks who I liked immediately. I got the sense that these folks loved taking care of our national parks, and that made me appreciate it all even more. The woman who checked me in explained that dogs had to be on leashes because of the bears. I told her I understood.

"Say, if we want to stay another night tomorrow, will we be able to do that at the same site?"

"Yes, definitely. In fact, with the snow coming in, you might have to stay here for a couple nights."

"Oh wow, okay. I hadn't thought of that."

She gave me a map and explained where everything was. There were no hookups but there was a sewage dump if needed and a payphone. No cell reception or Wi-Fi anywhere for miles.

I thanked her and went to park and set up our home. It was still sunny and a nice fall day when we parked. I put Hafa on his 30-foot leash to wander about nearby. He sniffed around, happy about our new location. And so was I. Though the campground had a lot of sites, they were mostly spread out, and less than half of them were occupied. Many people had driven cars up there and set up tents, tougher and more rugged folks than Hafa and me.

I tried starting the generator, but it wouldn't budge. I tried OB's tips, and still it wouldn't start. Must be because of the altitude and cold; it sounded like an engine that couldn't turn over. I'd have no electricity in the rig tonight, and with the power inverter out, I still couldn't use the TV at all. At least now I knew how to use the propane heater. And I wasn't in a tent. It could be good; it could be bad.

Hafa and I went for a walk. We passed a few other couples and families, all of them friendly and relaxed. One woman was walking her German shepherd, and so we let our dogs say hi and sniff each other for a few minutes. Both were young uncut males, so they sniffed apprehensively and then mutually backed away from each other.

About a half-mile from my campsite was a tiny convenience store with two payphones outside. I tied Hafa to the fence and went in to look around. The store had a small selection of snacks and drinks, and there was an older man with a bushy gray beard working the counter. I patted my pockets and realized that I'd left my wallet in the rig.

"Say, I need to get like $2 or $3 in quarters for the payphone."

"Oh, no problem," and the man went to open the register.

"I just left my wallet in the RV, and I'm parked a ways down, so I'll have to bring you the cash later."

"Oh, sorry, can't do that."

He tossed the change back in the register and closed it all in one fluid motion, a bit of theatrics. I'd figured I seemed good for $3, but I could tell he wasn't the type who negotiated once he'd said what's what.

"All right, I'll be back."

I took Hafa back down to the rig, grabbed my wallet and then turned around. When we got back, I tied Hafa to the fence and went back inside, bought two beers and changed $4 into quarters, then went out to the payphone and opened a beer. I brought Hafa over by the payphone, lit a cigar, dropped in some quarters and called my brother first. He answered, and I told him about the day's drive and how I wished he was still there. Then I let him know where I was and that I may get snowed in and not have reception for a couple days. I thought it would be safe to have a record of my whereabouts in case anyone needed to know. This wasn't necessary, but again, we usually think of ourselves as more important than we really are and being without your magic phone makes you feel so naked and strange.

Then I called two of my biggest clients and left both their assistants voicemails explaining that I was out of service, but if they needed anything in the next day they could email so and so and everything would be taken care of. I ran out of quarters, so then I tried to make a collect call to my friend Nic in Bozeman to let him know I was a day or two from him. He didn't answer, but then I read the instructions on the front of the phone. You could actually call the operator and give them your credit card number to charge if you didn't have quarters. I wasn't familiar with payphones. and I hadn't read the instructions.

So I went through the process, gave the operator my card number and the phone number I wanted to reach, and called OB. I complained about the generator and he said to keep trying. That it was probably adjusting to the altitude and colder weather. I wrote down notes of all of his tips for getting it to start, then went back to the RV to give it a go. I followed all of his advice, and still, the generator wouldn't start. I walked Hafa back to the payphone one last time and called Nic, with the help of the operator and a credit card.

Nic was relieved that I wasn't in jail.

"Who makes collect calls? Only prisoners make collect calls." He had already checked with all the local police stations to see if they had me after he got a missed collect call from me. "So you're at Yellowstone? How is it?"

"It's gorgeous, but the dog has to be on a leash and it's supposed to snow a lot, so we'll probably leave here tomorrow if we can and head your way."

"What entrance to Yellowstone are you by? I wonder if you should take the 89 or the 191."

"I don't know. I don't have any service or...Oh wait. I have a map."

I pulled a map I'd gotten out of my jacket. "Can you believe I'm calling from a payphone and using a real map?"

"You're really doing it."

I found myself on the map.

"Okay. I'm just a few miles from the west entrance."

"Oh sweet, you're only 100 miles from Bozeman then. You could come straight here or take the 287 and that goes right through Ennis. That's where we camped out last year when you were here with Rich and Erik. That'd be really nice."

"Oh really? I loved that place. Okay, I'll let you know what happens."

I hung up the phone and took Hafa back to our site and started a campfire. I put Hafa back on his 30-foot leash tied to the picnic table, and he sniffed around the site, smelling new kinds of animals and smells out there. And so did I. Though I hadn't chosen to completely unplug, I now was more unplugged than I'd been in a long time. No way to reach the outside world except for a payphone ten minutes up the road. I sat by the campfire, had a few drinks and reflected on the stresses I'd tried to leave behind back home. I noticed how serene and beautiful and quiet it was out there.

Once the fire died down, I took Hafa inside and put on some music. I made myself a sandwich and drank some more whiskey. I was starting to feel pretty isolated, with no power, no generator, no TV, no Wi-Fi, no cell reception.

I told Hafa, "I left town because I felt lonely and depressed at home; now I'm on my own out here and feel *really* lonely."

Hafa brought me his rope to play tug of war, his way of telling me to stop being so dramatic. He was here too, after all, and he wasn't so lonely. Dogs are not sentimental, but they love unconditionally.

"Yeah, buddy, we've got each other. I know."

Reflecting on past relationships, I conceded to myself that I had often been a selfish asshole and hadn't appreciated what I had while I had it. The women I had dated had all been great people with positive spirits who I was grateful to have known. I couldn't blame them or complain about their leaving, so I curled up with Hafa and tried to go to sleep, humming Tom Petty tunes to remind myself, "It's time to move on, it's time to get going."

MONTANA

WHEN WE WOKE UP AND WENT OUTSIDE, THE ground was covered in a foot of snow, and it was still coming down steadily. I took Hafa and walked up to the check-in area. There was a constant cascade of other campers heading up there for news about the roads. After a few minutes, a park ranger rode up on her snowmobile.

"How's it looking out there?" I asked her as she dismounted and walked toward us.

"Cold, getting colder." She walked up, and a crowd gathered around her for the update. "They're plowing the road to the west entrance and they should be opening the road in the next hour. If you're going to try to get out of here today, I'd go soon. Snow's just going to get worse and the roads will probably close back down."

I didn't feel like getting stuck there without a working generator, so I went back to the rig and made myself a coffee and fed Hafa. Then I pulled in the slides, pulled up the jacks and let off the brakes. We started out slowly.

I hadn't driven anything at all in years, let alone a bus, on snow. I didn't have chains or snow tires and kept imagining how easily I could start sliding and keep going.

As we pulled out of the campground, we waved goodbye to the park ranger and campground employees. They were all incredibly sweet and friendly. Regrettably, in my haste I left the 30-foot dog leash tied to my picnic table and buried under a foot of snow. I didn't mean to leave it, but I remembered once I was on the road and instantly regretted not leaving that campsite cleaner than I'd found it; I knew one of those nice park employees would have to pick it up for me.

ENNIS, MONTANA

THE ROADS THROUGH YELLOWSTONE TO THE WEST entrance were freshly plowed, but our caravan moved deliberately. I only went about 10 to 15 mph the whole way, and since I hadn't scraped or defrosted the windshield like anyone who is accustomed to driving in cold weather would have, I had a thick layer of ice and fog between me and the snowy road: total amateur move. When the road straightened out, there were a couple of trucks and cars that passed us, but we RVs were all moving at the same steady pace.

It took a while, but I finally went out through the west entrance of Yellowstone, and I was out in the world again and able to use my phone. As soon as we got out of the park, the roads weren't plowed, and as I made my way toward Ennis, there were a few semitrucks overturned on the sides of the road. Those long-haul truck drivers are fearless. Even after passing the wrecked ones, semis were passing me because I was driving too slow for them. The snow started coming down harder, and everything was white. My windshield still had ice on it that I could barely see through, and the highway was as pure white as everything else, with no indication of lanes or even turns in the road.

In the whiteout, I felt the beginnings of panic. I don't like driving in snow, and living in Southern California hasn't helped my abilities; again—not that I'd even owned a car in years. I passed a rest area for truckers and told myself I'd stop at the next one to take a break and make some fresh coffee, decompress and regroup. I was driving haltingly and couldn't see more than 10 feet ahead of the vehicle. Finally, I spotted another rest area sign and put on my left blinker and tapped the brakes. Slowing that machine down even from 15 mph made the rig turn to the left and then start sliding forward into the other lane. There were cars on the opposite side that I was turning left in front of, as well as a long row of cars that'd been stuck behind me. I could feel all of their jaws drop in anticipation of my RV tumbling into either them or the ditch as I skidded.

Trying to remain calm, I took a breath, made a few more easy taps on the brake, corrected the steering wheel and slid back in place to make the turn into the rest stop. The rest stop was really just a building with bathrooms and a large parking lot. I parked, turned on some coffee and poured myself a cup. I saw a trucker pull up and park, and I got out and started walking toward the building. I caught him on his way in to use the bathroom, wanting some expert advice. I hadn't driven in these circumstances before and the worst-case scenarios were on repeat in my mind. Truckers used these rest stops to park and sleep sometimes; I'm sure of it. Maybe I could set up camp there for the night and not have to drive through the blinding whiteout anymore.

"Hey! Excuse me."

I flagged the guy down. He seemed like he was in a rush to get to the bathroom but had enough time to answer one quick question. The wind was hard enough that we had to yell to hear each other, and it was freezing as the snow poured down like a Christmas morning.

"Yeah?"

"I'm in that RV over there and not used to driving in this stuff. You can park at these rest areas and sleep overnight, right?"

"Oh, I don't know. I don't stop; I drive for a living."

He hadn't really answered my question, but instead he made me feel like a worried baby for even asking it. "Where are you trying to get to?"

"I'm trying to get to Bozeman. Or even at least to Ennis."

"Ennis is only like 13 miles that way. I just came from that direction. The road clears up after a few more miles."

"Oh, okay, thanks."

"No problem, good luck."

He went inside to use the bathroom, and I went back to my rig to psych myself up to drive with half the confidence of that guy. I cleaned the windshield, turned the ignition, pulled back onto the highway and crawled my way toward Ennis, all the while passing cars and semis turned over in the ditches. There must have been a dozen of them. I thought to myself, *I don't stop; I drive for a living.*

It was a relief once I finally made it to Ennis. The drive had been hellish, and my body was sore from clenching my shoulders and holding the steering wheel so tightly. I parked in town, left Hafa in the rig, walked over to a place called Gravel Bar and ordered a burger and a beer. And then another beer. The bartender was a sweet lady who seemed like she'd probably always worked there. I sat on the corner of the bar; there were two middle-aged guys to my right and two mid-30s guys on my left. They all seemed to know each other, and they treated me like a stranger welcomed in from the cold.

The two guys on my right were talking about the weather and different accidents they'd seen or heard reported. One of them said a semitruck had turned over in front of one of the nearby highway on-ramps and it'd be a few hours before it opened back up.

"You think it'd be safe to drive into Bozeman from here today? In a big RV?" I pointed out the window to the RV to give them the full picture.

"In an RV you're probably better off waiting. You'd be taking the 84 East. The roads should clear back up tomorrow, but there is one steep pass you'd have to cross that'd be pretty rough tonight. Probably not great in an RV, to be honest."

"Ah, thanks, just as well. I drove out of Yellowstone this morning in the whiteout and it was hell driving in that. I was thinking about just going out to Valley Garden Campground up the street for the night anyway."

"Oh, Valley Garden, it's great."

My burger arrived, and I started eating. The two men on my right went back to talking with each other as I ate my late lunch. The guys on my left were laughing about something, so I listened to them and laughed along while I ate.

The guy on my left was lecturing the guy on his left. "You see, women only like a man with confidence."

"Yeah, is that why you've only gotten laid twice in your life?"

The guy on my left nodded and laughed, and they went on like this, and I kept laughing along.

The crowd of locals there were fun and good people. I said my goodbyes and went down the road to the campground to set up shop. There was one man near the stream with a pickup truck and a dog running around. He may have been there fishing, but about an hour after I parked, I saw him drive out of the park. Then I was the only person in the entire campground, and I let Hafa go explore while I set up a fire. That morning in Yellowstone had been his first time even seeing snow, and here, everything was covered in it. He ran around in circles in the snow, biting it and having the best day of his life once again.

There were signs posted on the picnic table advising us to watch out for grizzly bears. The last time I'd camped there with Nic, Erik and Rich, we'd seen a moose, a rattlesnake, beavers and some other critters. It was the first place that made me fall in love with Montana, and I was back here to show Hafa what it was all about. I was excited to get to see Nic and Jentry the next day. It kept snowing and, out in the dark cold by ourselves, I began to worry about the bears myself, so we put out the fire and went inside for the night. After a few tries, I got the generator to start and ran it for a couple hours to cook and watch a movie. I also found a spare fuse and was able to get the power inverter working again. I was back in business. For the evening's entertainment I picked the DVD of the 1980 classic *Airplane!*

"Wait a minute. I know you. You're Kareem Abdul-Jabbar."

BOZEMAN, MONTANA

AFTER WE WOKE UP IN ENNIS, HAFA WALKED AND sniffed around in the snow while I had a coffee. We waited until around 10 a.m. and the sun came out to clear the roads. There must have been more than a foot of snow stacked on top of the rig, and huge ice chunks had formed and caked themselves under the wheel covers and steps. I kicked off some of the ice from around the wheels, and Hafa got into the excitement of it all and tried to help bite and hit the ice chunks with his paws as well. Then we packed up camp and headed north up US-287 and then took MT-84 East to Bozeman.

There was one pretty steep mountain pass along the way, as the man at the bar had told me the day before, and I was grateful that I had waited an extra day to let the snow clear before making the hike. The drive the day before had been long enough on its own, and I'd gotten a picturesque and relaxing night's stay in Ennis. There was still a little snow and ice on the roads, so I drove slower than everyone else once again. The locals were used to this weather and I'm sure my driving annoyed them. There was a several-mile stretch where the road was one lane and I had a line of cars behind me. Occasionally, one would pass me and fly on down the road out of sight. One pickup truck honked as he passed me and I immediately honked back, surprising him. He kept driving and then was gone. A force of habit, anytime I'm driving and someone honks at me, I always honk back.

About a mile outside of downtown Bozeman, I found an RV park called Sunrise Campground. I parked by the entrance, and a man in his late 50s named Marty was just about to leave. He and his wife, Mary Joe, run the place, and he was on his way to give one of the other guests a ride into town but said he would check me in quickly before he left.

Marty had a real rugged Survivorman feel to him and gave me the rundown of the operation: codes to bathroom and Wi-Fi. He ran my credit card and gave me a receipt.

"I'll need to fill up on propane at some point too."

"Oh, you need propane? All right, let's do that now before you park and hook up." I could tell he was busy, but was the type of man who will put off his own needs to help someone else first.

He directed me on where to move the RV so he could fill up my propane. I parked and went around to open the compartment that housed my propane tank, but the compartment was frozen shut. I gave the handle a sturdy upward tug and half the handle broke off. Frozen, all right.

I put on my gloves and worked at the remaining half of the handle, determined that I needed to have propane. Finally, it clicked open and we were able to fill her up.

Then Marty hopped on a four-wheeler and had me follow him. He pulled up to a site and waved me in, showing me where to park. "The water lines froze over last night, but I'm going to turn them on now for a while if you need to fill up."

"Oh, thank you, sir. Say, I have a dog in here with me. Is it okay if he runs around a bit?"

"I don't care. My dog died."

I wasn't sure how to respond to that, really, but I knew we were done and he had places to be.

"I'm sorry to hear that."

"It's been two years. It's what they do. You love them and then they die."

I couldn't argue with that. But it was a damned depressing thing to say to a stranger. Marty left and I went into the RV to set up camp. I set the brakes, lowered the jacks and opened up the slides. I connected the electricity and went to fill up my freshwater tank. The hose that was in the compartment was only about 10 feet long, so it wouldn't reach the spigot. I looked around and my neighbor's water pump was close enough, so I quickly used theirs and filled the tank with water.

Now I had propane and water and a full tank of gas, so I decided to empty the sewage tanks as a matter of house cleaning. I opened the outer compartment that housed the tanks and set up the hoses to drain, then I went to pull the lever that drains the tanks. It wouldn't budge. It was at an awkward angle, but I tightened my grip and pulled up and *snap*. I'd broken half of this handle too. The tanks were frozen shut. The RV had a meter that would show you how full each thing was: propane, clean water, sewage and so forth. According to the meter, the sewage was full and needed to be drained.

Nic's fiancée, Jentry, sent me a text asking if I'd made it to Bozeman safely. I sent her back, "I'm in Bozeman setting up at RV park. Trying to empty my tanks." I put my phone down for a moment, then pulled it back out to add to my text, "Emptying the tanks of the RV. Not mine."

Luckily, the RV next to mine had a nice old man outside tinkering with his tanks too. His had been frozen, so he told me that he had boiled a few pots of water and poured them down the drain to thaw his frozen pipes. This had just worked for him a few moments ago, he claimed, and so I set about boiling pots of water and pouring them into my RV's pipes. This went on for 30 minutes until I finally got the tanks to drain. It was a relief since I needed to finish what I'd set out to do, and afterward, I felt a sense of accomplishment.

I went over to the men's bathroom and brought a bag with me so I could shower. I got out of the shower and realized I'd forgotten to bring a towel again. I used my dirty clothes to dry off, got dressed and took Hafa to a field there between the two highways. Big enough of an area for him to bounce around in the snow and relieve himself. While we were in the field, Nic pulled up in his Dodge Ram truck to pick me up. I put Hafa in the RV, left him some food and rode into town with Nic. It always feels like home when you reunite with good friends who you haven't seen in a while. Nic was especially proud of his new truck. We'd drive past another truck and they'd wave at each other.

"Everyone with a pickup truck waves at me now. This Dodge Ram 2500 turns so many heads of cowboy dudes up here. I finally know what it feels like to be a hot chick."

"Can you imagine if you had the 3500?"

Nic laughed, "No way, can't even imagine."

The last time I'd been to Bozeman, the year before, I'd met a bearded homeless man wearing several layers of coats on Main Street next to the bars. He looked like Jack Black, if Jack Black only slept outside and never trimmed his hair or beard. He was dressed in overalls and wore a cowboy hat. Maybe a mix of Jack Black and Stinky Pete from *Toy Story*.

"Hey man, you an actor?" He said it to me out of nowhere, I hadn't noticed him and I didn't really get it. I looked around to make sure he was talking to me. It was just the two of us outside on Main Street somehow.

"No, I'm not an actor. Are you an actor?"

He smiled and took a drag of his cigarette. "Yeah, I'm an actor. I'm always acting, man." He seemed so proud of that line, like he was setting it all up to be able to say that.

The guy was interesting, but it was cold, and I wanted

to get into the bar where my friends were, so I gave him a wave like I was trying to leave. "Okay. Nice to meet you; have a good one."

"All right man," he said as if he had more to say that I was missing out on. "I'll just be over here on this bench for the next 30 to 35 years."

I laughed and wondered if maybe he was an actor, and maybe there were hidden cameras somewhere. He had too much personality to be truly staying on that bench. Such a cold place to be homeless.

Nic drove us into town, and I wondered if I'd see that crazy kook on his bench again now, a year later.

Bozeman is a fun, small college town, with Montana State University and a population a little under 50,000. There are a few cowboy bars where you can usually find a poker game, and there are college bars with cute ladies. All on Main Street. Since it's Montana, the people aren't quite as arrogant or self-absorbed as you'd find in some big cities. Nic is always showing me new songs, and on the drive into town he played me "Goodbye Carolina" by the Marcus King Band.

"This guy singing is only 22 years old. Can you believe that?"

King was wailing on his guitar, and those lyrics...

Immediately, I added this to my playlist rotation for the road trip, and it's one of my favorite songs to this day. It seemed unreal that the voice singing those words was so young, yet sounded so powerful.

Nic took me to a bar, and we had a beer and caught up a little. Then we went to his house to pick up Jentry and their nine-week-old baby, Ruby. They hadn't left Ruby with a babysitter yet, so this dinner with me would be Jentry's first moments away from their newborn.

We dropped off Ruby at the newly hired babysitter's house, then went and had dinner. I told them about the road trip, and they told me about adjusting to life in Montana and life as parents. When I had last visited them, they were living in Manhattan and Jentry was working as a nurse practitioner. Somehow, Nic convinced her to move to Bozeman and raise their family there. He was in the process of starting a new company, and Jentry had a job lined up that she'd start in a couple weeks. They seemed happy, and it was fantastic to see friends again.

Jentry was curious to hear more about my plans for the trip.

"So, where do you go after Bozeman?"

"I don't know; I wanted to see my nephew, so I stopped in Provo. And I wanted to see you guys, so I stopped in Bozeman. I have the RV for another couple weeks, so I can go wherever, but this was the only real destination I had planned."

"Seriously?" She laughed, and Nic stepped in.

"Yeah, babe, some people like to live in the moment and not plan everything out."

She snarled at him, and it seemed like this was some sort of ongoing argument they had. I also felt bad for her since she didn't yet have a job or many friends in the area, stuck at home raising a baby while Nic was out at meetings and starting a business. In a few weeks, though, she was set to start her new job, and she's outgoing enough to make friends anywhere. Moving to a new city is tough on its own, and I don't have any kids, so I can't even imagine what all they were juggling.

Nic's new company that he was in the process of launching was an app called Land Trust that lets landowners list their properties to rent for hunting and fishing. He was making a new deal with a property in Billings that he needed to photograph for the app the next day and invited me to tag along and camp out for a night in Billings at the new property. He was going to go up in a small two-seater airplane to take aerial photos too, but there wouldn't be room for me in the plane. I told him that was just fine.

"Great, we'll leave at 8 a.m., and you can just follow me into Billings."

"That's a little early, and I doubt you want to drive as slow as me on the highway. How about I'll leave around 10 a.m. and meet you for lunch after you take pictures?"

So that was our plan. We went to pick up Ruby. Jentry did well but was obviously missing her baby after only an hour apart. I told her the story of the Chinese farmer that my brother had told me. "It could be good; it could be bad."

They dropped me back at the RV park, and I took Hafa for another walk and poured myself a drink. Then I put on the movie *High Fidelity* with John Cusack. While watching it, I couldn't help but replay my past relationships in my mind, and found myself trying to list out my own top five heartbreaks. I could only come up with a top four, but maybe someday the list will get longer. As usual, the last one hurt the most and was all I could think about as I tried to go to sleep.

I don't know how people who are more well-adjusted handle breakups, but I often change some of my behaviors or drop activities I had embraced while with that person. For instance, my ex-girlfriend who had been my excuse for taking the trip often ate sunflower seeds, and so I would eat them sometimes when she did, and I enjoyed them fine. Since we'd broken up, I hadn't eaten any sunflower seeds and had no plans to. They remind me of her, and I prefer to block that out since she's no longer in my life, and even the briefest memory of her could potentially bring a moment of sadness, which I am ostensibly too fragile to allow myself. It seems absurd, but I think I've done this plenty of times, whether consciously or not.

When I was married, we'd often drink maté tea together a few times a day, a traditional Argentinian activity. It was a daily practice that essentially ended for me the day that relationship ended. I don't know if this wiping clean of the routine slate is healthy or helpful for the soul at all, but lying there on the couch in the RV next to Hafa, watching John Cusack wax on about his breakups made me think about such things.

BILLINGS, MONTANA

BY THE TIME I LEFT BOZEMAN, THE SUN WAS UP AND the snow had completely gone from the roads. Billings was 141 miles east on I-90. Finally I was driving as fast as the speed limit again, and the roads felt safe, so I turned on "Goodbye Carolina" loud on the speakers on repeat for at least an hour. A little way out from Bozeman the wind picked up and was sending the entire rig to and fro several feet at a time like a sailboat caught in a storm. A few miles would go by and I'd be fine, and then a WHOOSH of wind and I'd find myself steering back into the wind, countering as much in one direction as it was pushing us in the other. I turned the music down and clenched up again, hunkered over the steering wheel. If the issue wasn't snow, it was wind.

About halfway through the drive, another gust came out of nowhere and WHOOSH, the whole rig sailed in an instant from the right lane to the left. I've heard it's not uncommon for big rigs to tumble over from heavy wind, but I also figured we weighed enough to keep that from happening. I quickly moved back into my own lane. Luckily there wasn't another car nearby, but right at that moment a fox crossed the highway right ahead of me. I moved my foot over to tap the brakes, but didn't want to cause an accident over this. I already had this damned wind to deal with. The fox was responsible for himself.

The rig was still doing over 60 and the fox moved forward more, right in front of us, and then he looked at me. All but daring me. He looked me right in the eyes, I swear. Then, just as we came within a few feet of him, he darted to my right and was off the highway. He was as quick and sly as they come, and I was glad. Driving over a fox couldn't be a good omen, and I didn't want that hanging over me. I got off the highway in Big Timber to get gas and coffee and shake my legs after the scare with the wind and the fox.

I was gaining more and more respect for long-haul truck drivers who did this day in and day out, going from one kind of weather to the next. The rest of the drive became easier, and then I drove into Billings, the largest city in Montana, at 100,000 people. It was noon and Nic had texted me the name of the restaurant we were going to meet at, a steak house called Jake's. I found the restaurant but had to navigate around five blocks away before I found street parking where I could fit the rig downtown. I gave Hafa some food and water, and locked him in the Southwind.

Jake's is a classic steak house with wood floors, wood paneling and great food; it's been there since the early

1980s. When I got there, I found Nic at a table with two other gentlemen. One was the pilot who'd flown Nic that morning to take aerial photographs for his new app company. The pilot looked to be in his late 40s; he was a friend of the landowner and an avid hunter, so he'd offered to take Nic up to take the pictures. He was dressed more like he had just been golfing. They were only in the sky for a few minutes before Nic told him he was going to throw up, and they had to come back down. Flying in those small two-seaters is a different experience than in a commercial jet, and Nic's stomach didn't agree with it.

The other guy at the table was Colter. He, Nic, and I were all 31 at the time. Colter had grown up in that area, a sixth-generation Montana rancher. He had been helping to make introductions for Nic to other landowners who could work with his company and had made the intro for the property we were visiting later that day.

We all had beers, except for Colter, who had an iced tea, and the food came and was delicious. I was sitting next to the pilot, and there was a pair of guys at the table behind us. At one point, one of them turned around and tapped the pilot on the shoulder.

"Hey! I thought that was you," the guy at the other table told the pilot and stuck out his arm to shake his hand.

After some explanation, I learned that the pilot had an accident a little over a year before, and the guy at the other table was one of the first paramedics to arrive on the scene.

"We didn't think you were going to make it when we showed up. We gave you maybe a 2% chance of surviving."

They talked a bit more, and then the guys at the other table left.

A year and a half before, the pilot had been out hunting on the same land we were going out to that night and was with his son. He had a shotgun in case they ran into coyotes or anything, and he got on his four-wheeler with his son, putting the shotgun on his seat with the barrel facing outward. On the property, there are a number of gates with cattle guards on them.

As he was driving the four-wheeler, doing around 15 mph, he went over a cattle guard and the vehicle went to an immediate halt. The two back wheels jumped up, and somewhere in the shuffle, the shotgun came dislodged from under him and caught on something to make it cock and then fire from directly under him. The pilot was shot in the balls, and the bullets moved up into his abdomen. Lying on the ground in the kind of misery I can't even fathom, he was able to send his 12-year-old son to go call for help.

The man had shot his own balls off. No joke. They airlifted him out with exceptionally low odds of surviving, but here he was eating lunch with us. If I hadn't heard the story, I wouldn't have known he'd had any major accidents. And if the paramedic hadn't been sitting right behind us at that steak house that day, I wouldn't have ever known the story at all.

After lunch, we drove out to the ranch. Seventeen thousand acres of land about 20 miles north of Billings that Nic would be signing up to his company in order to let hunters pay to book days there. Once we went into the first gate, the road became less paved and more rock and gravel, so I drove carefully while following Nic in his truck. He pointed out his window. I looked, and there was a herd of deer out in the field. Nic is always on the lookout for such things. Then we passed a hill with several guys set up with guns, using the area as a shooting range since there was a hill that would prevent any stray bullets. There must have been a dozen small groups of people out there a few hundred yards apart from each other, practicing with all sorts of rifles.

A few miles later, we went through another gate and the road became more dirt than gravel. Then after passing one more gate, we got to the house and barn where the guy who oversees the place stays. He was some sort of retired specials ops guy. Who knows what that guy had seen in his life. He was friendly but brief and suggested we park on the pavement by the barn, as we could hook up to electricity there. I moved the rig over to the barn, set the brakes, lowered the jacks and opened the slides. I let Hafa out of the rig, and he was astounded by the breadth of freedom we had there.

We were parked about 100 feet from the fence and cattle guard where the pilot had accidentally castrated himself. We plugged in the power, pulled out some beers and lawn chairs, and set up a ring of rocks to build a fire in. The way Nic built our campfire in Billings was textbook. While

I was a Boy Scout when I was young, Nic is a practiced and true outdoorsman who puts me to shame in such matters. He had his ax out, shearing kindling from the edges of the firewood and using the little strips of kindling to build the foundation for the fire with care, like a tiny log cabin. Nic had the fire lit and roaring within minutes, but went about his business as though it were his job, steadied and focused on the task at hand. He wasn't boastful about the quality of the fire, but I think he certainly could have been.

Nic had brought his dog too, and planned to do some pheasant hunting in the morning. His dog was a black Labrador retriever named Jake. Jake had graduated training for bird hunting, was an attentive and obedient dog and was also a little older and wiser than Hafa.

While Hafa is a smart dog, he is certainly not yet wise. Wisdom only comes from a certain amount of experience, and he is still young. We walked around some of the property and Hafa was introduced to the livestock. The cows would stand still and moo, and Hafa would run around in circles at full speed. To tire out the dogs, I tossed six or seven tennis balls around and kept throwing them. Both dogs wanted to retrieve each one, and at some point they began chasing after the same ball at the same time, and Hafa growled and barked at Jake like a complete asshole. Since I had trained my dog, I thought that he must be a gentle pacifist that would naturally share his toys.

I made a loud "Pssssst!" noise and snapped at Hafa.

Then I tried throwing a few balls at a time, but they

still chased after the same one, and Hafa went straight in for the attack, snarling and biting Jake's back between his shoulders. In a moment, they were suddenly growling and barking and biting at each other, circling in a cartoon-like mix of shuffling. I ran over and broke them up and smacked Hafa in the face and told him all sorts of serious threats about this behavior, then grabbed him by the collar and sat him down. I'd had this dog since he was eight weeks old, and here he was six months later attacking another dog. My friend's dog. Never had I seen him act out in this way, but food and toys are the two most common ways to start a dog fight. Raw primal aggression.

I presume that the adrenaline and amount of freedom he was enjoying had made him act out like an overactive child learning their boundaries. I'd overseen all of Hafa's formal training personally, so even though dogs will be dogs, this one mishap still made me feel like a failed teacher. German shepherds in particular are naturally territorial and protective, so I'm sure being a nomad made it confusing to Hafa as to what he should even be protecting at that point. We go to extraordinary ends to make sense of the actions of those we care about.

"Hey, if you're going to leave him outside, you need to put the shock collar on him."

Nic had a shock collar for Jake that was used in his training for hunting birds. If I were in his shoes and another dog had attacked mine, I think I would have been defensive and upset. Nic stayed cool and made his condition clear right then. Either Hafa stayed in the RV or wore the shock collar.

I paused and thought with my head down for a minute before I answered, "All right, where's the collar?"

The idea of shock collars had always bothered me. Nic assured me of their efficacy, so we put the collar on Hafa, and with the push of a button on a remote, I could send him a slight jolt if he did anything out of line again. I picked up the tennis balls and put them away to get rid of any incentives for dispute.

Hafa went near Jake again to badger him, and we gave him a quick *bzzz*, set at a low intensity. Hafa jumped back like a scared cat. I asked Nic to text me a link to the brand and model so I could buy one of these for when I was back home.

Jake had a bite-sized chunk of hair missing from his shoulder, but no blood had been drawn. As ashamed as I was for raising such a monster that would be capable of this sort of confrontation, it's all just something that happens. Dogs will fight sometimes, even if you raise them to be pacifists with great care and affection. Hafa wagged his tail and kept following Jake around with his tongue out, like an annoying kid trying to play with someone older who has no interest, and as a scolded dog showing no signs of admitting he was at fault.

We flirted with the idea of playing a game of chess. Nic hadn't played before, and I offered to teach him, but his idea of camping didn't include having to learn something new. In his view, go out in nature to turn your mind off and relax, so we had a valid reason to hang out by the campfire and chat over cigars and drinks instead.

"*This* is camping," I told him.

"Yeah, *this* is camping."

Nic and I had another beer and started cooking up steaks in my cast-iron skillet. We were about to eat when Colter, from our lunch earlier that day, pulled up in his truck. We'd invited him to pop by but weren't sure if he would. We all three had started our own companies and were all the same age. Colter was working on an app that had to do with boondocking and booking places to stay in an RV, so he also wanted to ask me about my particular experiences on my trip so far. I'm not sure how much of a startup tech scene is in the Billings area, so I thought it might be refreshing for Colter to chat about business ideas with both of us. Just like it was refreshing for me to hang out with them.

Colter said he was sober, so he didn't drink. I gave him a can of carbonated flavored water, and Nic and I switched to some sort of expensive tequila. Colter had brought his dog too, a small poodle mix. Hafa antagonized her with attention as well, but playfully. Colter talked about his app and taught me some tips for boondocking and the RV lifestyle. We talked about camping, hunting and business. After the sun set, Colter left, and Nic and I kept drinking tequila by the fire.

Nic planned on checking out the pheasant hunting on

the property the next morning. Since his company was focused on renting out properties for hunting, they needed to follow all the rules, and I didn't have a hunting license in Montana. With these facts at play, I decided I'd sleep in the next morning while Nic went hunting. We drank a good amount of tequila that night, and then Nic went to sleep by around 10 p.m. A night away when you have a newborn at home must provide a kind of oasis of extra needed rest.

Nic slept on the fold-out couch in the RV, and I stayed out by the fire for a while longer. My mind kept circling around my business and life back home, the reality of bills and obligations. Then I thought about my ex-girlfriend and felt bad and lonely for myself, and I thought about the dogs fighting and being upset with Hafa for attacking Jake. When I finally lay down in my bed, I couldn't shut off these thoughts or keep my eyes closed. I lay there most of the night, unable to sleep. Around the time the sun came up and I heard Nic go out to hunt, I finally dozed off for two or three hours. Then I got up, made coffee and started cleaning up our fire pit, and unhooked the electricity from the rig.

Nic came back empty-handed from his hunt, and we met some of the ranch hands who gave us more details about the property, pointing at things and telling us how the property's 17,000 acres extended so far in this direction or that. We tidied up after ourselves, making sure that we left the site cleaner than we'd found it, then headed out. On our way toward the main gate, we saw the pilot pulling up in his truck. We all got out and talked for a few minutes about the different animals we had or hadn't seen the past day. As we left, he and his son were heading into the same property to do some hunting of their own. Nothing could stop this guy from going hunting as often as possible, even in the same place where the tragedy occurred.

The drive back to Bozeman was windy again, but not as bad as the first time. I went back to the same RV park I'd been at before, checked in and parked back in the same spot I'd been in two nights ago. Something about the couple that ran the place, Marty and Mary Joe, made me feel at home. Despite only having a few conversations with them, I decided that they were two of the nicest folks I'd ever met, and I was glad to be a returning patron to their park.

No more open fields and wide expanse of space and freedom for Hafa and me. No more 17,000 acres off on our own on a ranch somewhere. But Marty and Mary Joe gave me a warm family vibe that I thought was just fine. Once I had set up the rig, I used the camp's laundry room to clean some of my clothes and then took a shower. For the first time on the trip, I remembered to bring a towel with me to the shower.

BOZEMAN, PART 2

BY THE TIME I FINISHED MY LAUNDRY, NIC HAD texted me the name of a brewery in Bozeman they wanted to meet at for dinner and drinks. I walked and fed Hafa, then locked him in the RV and called myself an Uber. I made sure to wear my Pettijohn Construction hat so that I'd blend in.

My driver was some friendly college kid who wouldn't stop talking for one minute. A road would be closed off, and he'd go on about how the road being closed was going to affect the drop-off time, then he'd ponder aimlessly out loud about why the road might be closed. And then a train came, and we sat at the traffic light waiting for the train to pass, and he went on about how long the train was taking and apologized for all the delays.

"No worries, there's no rush," I kept telling him, thinking it would calm him down. But he kept talking and going on for the whole drive like he needed to unload everything that came into his mind. I think he was an MSU student trying to earn some money outside of classwork. He had nothing to say, but he couldn't shut up. The ride took less than ten minutes, but he must have apologized about how long it'd taken no less than five times.

When I walked into the brewery, I found a large round booth with Nic, Jentry and Ruby, as well as three of their friends. There was a married couple I had met on my last trip to Montana, Ryan and Anna, and another guy named Blake who I hadn't met before. I'd been to this brewery with Nic and Jentry on my last trip to Bozeman as well, but I was much less hungover this time and could actually enjoy it. The food and beers were great, and everyone was in a fun mood.

Blake had lived in New York City until recently as well, until Nic invited him to come out to Bozeman and offered him a job with his new company. When Blake came and visited, he fell in love with the Montana lifestyle and ended up staying, though he took a job with a different company in town instead of joining the one Nic was starting.

We all talked and told each other stories for a while. Since I knew that Ryan participated in sharpshooter competitions and had a handful of custom guns, I asked him, "Hey, if I want to buy a gun around here somewhere, where should I go, and what should I get?"

"For a guy like you, you just need a Glock. That's probably what you should get. There's a website called armslist.com—I would just go there. But where are you off to next?"

I showed them all the rough itinerary of a map I had on my phone.

"I'm not sure. Where should I go after Bozeman?" I knew I wanted to head in the direction of Mount Rainier in Washington, but I didn't have a specific plan.

Ryan looked at my route on the app on my phone, then told me with confidence, "You should stay a night in Coeur d'Alene. It's absolutely gorgeous there. It's beautiful. Like, really beautiful."

Ryan is a burly, manly man with a big beard, but as he called Coeur d'Alene beautiful, I could see his eyes glistening like an excited child. I had asked him for advice on where to go next, and I believed his answer right away.

The others at the table nodded and mumbled in agreement, but I hadn't even heard of this place before. "Is that in Idaho?"

Nic chimed in, "Oh yeah, I forgot about Coeur d'Alene. You'll like it there."

Ryan went on, "Yeah it's at the top skinny section of Idaho. You can camp out by the lake; it's kind of hard to explain why it's so nice there, but it just is. The whole town is built around a really big lake. I'd definitely go there if I were you. It's beautiful."

"All right, I trust you. Coeur d'Alene it is. I'll look it up and go there next." I wrote the name down in the notes app on my phone so I could remember the instructions.

Blake looked at my map itinerary as well. "Oh, Yosemite..." He said that and then appeared to reflect on it for a minute. And then, "I've never been much of a religious person, but I went to Yosemite alone one time on a road trip, and there was something about that place that actually made me feel really spiritually connected, not to sound cheesy. There's something about it all that makes you feel awe and wonder, like you're just a speck in the shadow of those big trees."

I could hardly believe it, but he said it all very seriously. Actually, I was happy to hear such things.

"Man...I've been to Sequoia National Park before and seen the big trees, but I've never been to Yosemite, so that's one of the stops I'm really excited about."

"Oh, the big redwoods. Man, it's so beautiful there. It made me feel some kind of connection with the universe. I'm serious."

We paid our tab and all decided to go back to Nic and Jentry's home to play some card games. We got there and they let me hold Ruby. Holding a newborn baby is always a whole experience and feels like you're in charge of protecting this precious cargo. She smiled at me, and I smelled and kissed her new forehead. Jentry snapped a photo of me holding Ruby, then she went and put her to bed.

The six of us played Cards Against Humanity and kept drinking. We all had each other laughing and cracking up the whole time. Jentry laughed so hard it sounded like she was crying and out of air, and then the next round she would laugh just as hard again. I think this was the most she'd drunk since before getting pregnant over a year ago. It seemed like we all needed the drinks and laughter, and after a few hours we finally decided to call it a night.

Nic and Jentry were ready for bed, and I convinced Blake to drive me out to a bar for one drink so I wouldn't have to go out alone. We were the only two single guys there, so we were the only ones allowed to go out. Ryan and Anna went home, and we left at the same time as them.

"Just one drink; I'm supposed to go hunting at 6 a.m. tomorrow."

"Just one," I assured him, and then we went down to Main Street.

It was the night of MSU's homecoming football game, so most of the bars were packed and rowdy. We ordered some tall Guinness beers and approached a booth with four women in it. Blake introduced us, and then we both invited ourselves to sit down and chat. We quickly had them laughing and having fun, but Blake and I noticed they were all drinking water. Most likely they'd already gone too hard and were all getting tired and wanting to sober up and go home.

"We got here an hour too late," Blake told me as we went to order another beer. "Just one more."

After a few more drinks, we decided to leave so he could still wake up in time to go hunting. Blake went home and I met up with a woman named Ty, who came back to the RV park and stayed the night with me. Since I'd been in Bozeman a couple days earlier, I'd gotten to swipe around on a dating app and had already matched with Ty. After a few exchanges, she agreed to meet and then come back to the RV park. It seemed like a risk for any girl to take, going back to an RV park with some guy who's driving through. But she said yes, and we had a good night.

Dating apps have been a blessing for those who aren't social or outgoing enough, or perhaps lazy. Even when I go out to bars at home, I seldom go out alone and for whatever reason am often too shy to approach anyone. Dating apps have, over the past few years, simplified soulmate searching to the lowest common denominator. The never-ending flow of the swiping, window-shopping experience of online dating apps can also lead to analysis paralysis, of too many options for any reasonable person. That isn't at all to say that wonderful people aren't on these apps. Quite the contrary. I met my last three serious relationships on dating apps, including my ex-wife. And I'm honestly a better person because of those relationships. On the other hand, meeting someone by chance out in real life can seem more natural and by way of fate. I guess. Maybe.

In the case of the most recent relationship, by which I was still feeling wounded, we had connected on a dating app initially. We saw each other a few times, but then I left town on a month-long trip, and when I came back she was seeing someone else. A few months later I ran into her at a concert, and she had just broken up with the guy she had been seeing.

I rarely go into Hollywood anymore. That night I was with some buddies, and one of them had randomly come into the possession of four VIP tickets to an EDM show that night at the Palladium, so we ended up stopping by. At the show, we went backstage and to the VIP area, and one of my buddies said he detected a "a two spot" and had me follow him through 200 feet of crowds before coming up to two women who he thought we should hit on. I thought his eyesight must have been astounding to be able to spot these two from so far away, in such a dark and crowded venue. One of the women turned around, and I recognized that it was her. We connected once because of an app and then again in person, and we ended up talking most of that night instead of listening to the music.

Given how rarely either of us ever attended such events, it was like fate had reunited us, and after that night we started dating. I really believed the universe was pushing us together—for a while at least.

In any case, I met Ty on a dating app in Bozeman on the Saturday night of MSU's homecoming, and we hit it off. She was a student at MSU, living on campus at the dorms. A cute and free-spirited brunette, which feels like a typical way to describe a woman, but I've never heard of any man being described as free-spirited. In any case, she was. She had a few tattoos and wore glasses and was sweet and asked a lot of questions. We had a fun night, and by the next day Ty and I had both agreed that we enjoyed each other's company a lot, so I gave her the same offer I'd given to my brother.

"If you want to join me for a few days, you could come along with me and the dog, and then I could book you a flight from somewhere along the way back to Bozeman."

She took a moment to think, but then I remembered that I had already made that same offer the night before.

"Yeah, you said that last night. What city are you going to next?"

I had to pull out my phone and check my notes from the dinner the night before.

"Hmmm...I know it's on the way to Washington. It's a place called Coor Daleen?"

I struggled to pronounce it, but she knew what I meant. Her eyes lit up, even.

"I grew up in Coeur d'Alene! That's where my family is. You know, I've actually been thinking about taking some time off from school. Or maybe even taking the year off so I can travel. I'm not really sure what I want to do."

"You could show me the way there. Shouldn't cost much to fly you back, and I can just book the flight with points. Would be like two or three more days together and you're back before the end of the week."

I was surprised that she was considering it, though I often say yes to last-minute adventures myself. But she wanted to think and talk to her mom.

"Let me think about it. I'll text you."

After coffee, I drove her back to her university, pulling through the parking lot in this enormous rig and dropping her off at the dorms. She said she'd text me what she decided within a couple hours, which worked for me because I was off to meet Nic, Jentry and Ruby for a late breakfast.

It was close to 10 a.m. or so when I met back up with Nic

and family. We had some biscuits and gravy and laughed about the night before. I told them how much fun Blake is and that I was glad they had someone like that to hang out with in Bozeman. They invited me to come by their house to shower and rest before hitting the road. The first really nice shower I'd had since leaving home.

When I got out of the shower, I had a text from Ty that she'd accepted my offer and wanted to come along with me for a couple more nights, to as far as Coeur d'Alene, and then fly back to Bozeman. I was surprised and elated. Her school's semester had just started, yet she was ready for a break. A road trip seemed to scratch her travel itch the same as it had mine.

She said that she needed to pack and shower and that I could pick her back up at 2 p.m. at the same spot where I'd dropped her off. I got cleaned up and had a cigar in the backyard with Nic. He had a nice home and family and life all worked out in this land, and I envied it in many ways. He had a backyard where his dog could relieve himself and Nic could smoke a cigar, and no neighbors would even think about complaining. If it weren't for the frigidly cold winters, I could live in Montana. In the other seasons, it is a paradise that I'll always happily visit. But those four months or so make it impossible for me.

I said my goodbyes to Nic and Jentry, and I drove to a nearby station to fill up on gas, firewood, bottled waters and beer. Since I couldn't find my sunglasses, I bought a $5 pair of aviators at the gas station, then drove back over to the MSU campus to pick up Ty. Apparently, I had left my sunglasses in Blake's car the night before when we went out to the bars.

When I pulled into the parking lot to pick up Ty, Hafa cocked his head at me as if second-guessing my decision.

"You'll understand when you're older, buddy. Trust me."

She was sitting on a bench with her backpack on, ready to go.

CLINTON, MONTANA

FROM BOZEMAN TO COEUR D'ALENE, IT'S 366 MILES going northwest on I-90. I told Ty how I'd been deciding where to stop each night and told her how we should just try to get about halfway to Coeur d'Alene and then decide on a place to stop based on intuition and timing.

"We'll find the right campground, or it'll find us," I told her.

She nodded and smiled.

"All right, let's go!" She was excited and energetic, breathing new life into the adventure.

I love the type of people who jump in and say yes like that, so Ty was my kind of person, and I told her as much.

"You know, when I first moved to LA, I met a television director named Gary and went over to his house in Hollywood one time. He had a nice house with a big backyard that was fenced in and had a pool and a guest house and all of that. His wife and kids were inside the house while

Gary and I chatted in the backyard, and I played with his dog near the pool."

"That sounds nice."

"Yeah, it was. And I said to him, 'Gary, if I had a backyard like this with a pool, I'd be in that pool every day.' And Gary turned to me and very seriously said, 'I don't do anything *every* day.'"

"Ha ha, I like that. I don't do anything *every* day."

"Yeah, he made me realize that sometimes you have to say yes and try something new. If you do the same thing every day, then that's no good."

This made Ty smile. She had mixed up her routine even more impulsively than I had, and I respected her dearly for it.

Someone once showed me a 2013 documentary called *McConkey*, about professional skier and BASE jumper Shane McConkey. They demanded that I watch it, and if you haven't seen it, I demand that you watch it as well. Shane McConkey went to work every day *stoked* about every day of his life and, in my opinion, he serves as the ultimate example of saying yes and living each day in the moment.

Since Ty was more of a country girl than I'm used to meeting in LA, I could play country music, and both of us would sing along. There's no telling how many times I played "American Kids" and "Goodbye Carolina" that day. Ty was a fun co-pilot, and Hafa liked having her around, though he was now relegated to sitting between the seats or on the floorboard rather than sitting up in the passenger seat like he had been. In any case, he was getting twice as much attention.

We were entering Clinton, Montana when it started looking like sunset was approaching. We'd want to pick a site and set up a campfire before it got dark. I had Ty download a BLM app to her phone so she could look for some public land for us to park on. The app showed different color-shading on the topography to represent different types of land use, and there wasn't any real explanation of which roads to take. We tried to use the location pin on the phone and other map apps to find the right roads, but we ended up driving down farmland and right up to someone's driveway.

We were confused and lost, but we had the windows open and were driving slowly. Every so often, we'd see a group of deer galloping through the open fields like they were on adventures of their own. The sun was starting to set, and the property we were trying to reach looked like it was on the other side of these farms with no apparent public access roads. We turned the rig around and drove back toward where we'd exited the highway. Ty looked up a gas station we'd passed to navigate us back there and ask an employee for directions.

"This gas station says they have groceries there too. And they're highly rated for fried chicken," she said and laughed. This gas station in the middle of nowhere was locally famous for its fried chicken. The population of Clinton is about 1,000 people.

So we doubled back to this gas station in the middle of nowhere that's highly rated for fried chicken. We went inside and asked a few employees if they knew where any BLM land was for camping. The two women working the registers shrugged and pointed us to some of the free publications by the front door. There were some quarterly magazines about hunting and fishing, but nothing with a map of this area. We went out front and I gassed up the rig, hoping someone would come along who knew something.

It wasn't long before some guy parked a truck and started walking inside, so Ty and I cut him off to ask his advice. He was wearing a shirt that said "Clinton, Montana," which I thought was a good sign.

"Excuse me, sir. Do you know where any BLM land is around here, where we can park and camp at for the night?" I pointed at the RV so he got a clear picture.

The guy lifted both hands and kind of motioned in all directions. "BLM land? Well, it's everywhere. I mean, it's *everywhere*."

"Well, we have a map that says there's some thataway, but it was all private roads and farms, so we came back here. Thought we should ask a local for advice."

The guy took a moment and scratched his chin. "Well, let me think. I live up the road that way and have 600 acres. You could camp there."

Ty and I looked at each other like, "Of course this guy has 600 acres right up the street."

Then he proceeded to explain how to find a fishing spot

that was only a few miles away. He told us there'd be a sign for the river and for fishing access.

"I don't think camping overnight is allowed, but I've done it in my camper before, and no one ever bothered me about it."

"Sounds perfect; we'll go there. Thank you; have a good night, sir."

And we were off, determined to get set up and start a campfire before dark.

When we found the fishing area, there were, sure enough, signs with rules including "no fireworks" and "no dogs" and "no overnight camping." I pulled the RV around to the riverbank and, aside from one road nearby, we were the only people around for miles. We were parked about 15 feet away from the river and the only way to even see us from the road was on the one bridge that went over the river downstream.

We set up camp quickly, and I found enough rocks nearby to build a pit for the fire. Once I'd had a few beers and the fire was hot, I started chopping onions, garlic and potatoes, adding the chopped mix into tin foil with butter and seasonings, tossed that straight into the fire and set a timer for 45 minutes on my phone to indicate the ideal time to remove the potatoes. Campfire potatoes like how my brother had made them in Utah. Like how our dad used to make them.

Then I did the dishes and rubbed two steaks with seasoning and cooked them in my cast-iron skillet. The food came out pretty well. The steaks were a solid medium-rare, and the beers relaxed me from another day of driving. Ty's company relaxed me even more.

We sat out by the campfire after dinner and watched Hafa run up and down the riverbed, jumping in and biting at the water's splashes that he was causing. I'd try to towel him off before going inside, but as soon as we came back out, he was back in the water and covered in mud again.

I told Ty, "*This* is camping."

"This *is* camping," she repeated back with her youthful spiritedness.

We enjoyed the fire while listening to the stream a few feet away. I had a cigar, and we talked about our lives and families and things. We were still learning all of the basic details about each other.

After a while, we put out the fire and went inside. I'd been telling her about *Caddyshack*, and she said she hadn't seen it but wanted to. When I went to look for the DVD I couldn't find it in my collection, though, so I put on *Detroit Rock City* instead. We only watched a few minutes before pausing the movie to make love. Literally two minutes after we'd finished and were lying wrapped together in a naked silence, there was suddenly a *boom, boom, boom*—three loud knocks on the door. We turned and looked at each other, confused. I apprehensively got to my feet, still naked, then *boom boom boom*—three more loud knocks and now a flashlight shining through the window.

"Sheriff's department."

Finally, they announced themselves and I relaxed for a moment and put on some sweatpants. For a split second I had imagined some crazed *Deliverance*-type situation, so the police at least made sense for a midnight knock at the door, way out in nature. I knew we weren't supposed to park there overnight. I threw on my Carhartt jacket and cracked open the door, with my hair crazed and no shirt on.

The light from their flashlights hit me in the face and I couldn't see anything, standing on my top step, barefoot and dazed.

"Can you step on outside, please?"

"Ugh, yes, just let me grab some shoes."

I hustled back inside, then came back out and closed the door behind me. It was still muddy and cold out, and I was awkwardly holding my jacket shut since I wasn't wearing a shirt underneath. I could feel myself start to shiver and shake from the cold. As my eyes adjusted, I could recognize two men in sheriff's gear holding flashlights, with their SUV parked nearby. The way I was clutching my jacket closed must have spooked them. The one that was in charge was the first to talk to me.

"You have any weapons on you, sir?"

They looked ready to draw and fire on me as he said this. Suddenly I was nervous again, as I remembered that the police definitely terrify me.

I let go of my jacket, motioned to my lack of a shirt and clarified, "No, just no shirt. I'm cold."

"What are you doing out here?"

"Sorry, we just wanted to crash somewhere for a few hours. I thought this was BLM land, but the location pin on my phone was wonky. I asked a local at the gas station with the fried chicken, and he directed us here. Said he's camped here before overnight, so I just was trying to follow a local's advice."

I tried to sound rational, but my appearance and shaky nervousness made it a tougher sell.

"Anyone else out here with you?" The one in charge was still doing all of the talking.

"Just my girlfriend and my dog."

Calling her my girlfriend made more sense than explaining that we'd just met and were out here trespassing together. If they'd asked me, I couldn't even have told them her last name.

"Girlfriend." He said it as more of a statement than a question. Then he added a question, "Where are you coming from?"

"Bozeman" I answered quickly. "On our way to Coeur d'Alene."

"You have your driver's license?"

"It's inside; I could go grab it, no problem."

I moved toward the door, but he held his hand up, like the *stay* command for a dog, which stopped me in my tracks.

"That's fine. Just give me your name and date of birth."

He pulled out a pad and pen and wrote down my information, then started back toward their cruiser to run my info.

"Watch him," he said as he walked away.

"Sure," the other guy responded.

It seemed like overkill to me. What did they need to watch me for? In case I dive into the river?

I finally relaxed a bit, knowing I had a clean record and there weren't any outstanding warrants or records or anything for them to get disagreeable about. This was going pretty well, all things considered. Nothing beyond camping overnight in a day-use-only fishing spot.

I chatted with the other officer, who seemed less in charge, while his partner was running my info. I defended my reasoning a few more times and told him how I'd only made a campfire pit and was planning to put the rocks back in the morning and leave the place cleaner than I found it and so forth.

He shone his flashlight around the area and agreed with me, saying, "Yeah it's about as clean out here as it ever gets in the summer."

The other sheriff's officer came back, satisfied with my identification. My California license plate and driver's license had caught up with me, finally, and made me stick out.

He asked, "So what, are you on a big road trip across the country or something?"

"Yeah, I was in a funk and thought I should go out and clear my head for a while, so I rented the RV. My girlfriend is from Coeur d'Alene and is just going with me as far as there. My dog and I are traveling around all month, a German shepherd puppy inside there. Got inspired by *Travels With Charley*—the Steinbeck novel where he travels around America with his dog."

They liked all of this and smiled. In Montana, I suspect many people have read that book or that it may be required reading in their schools. The way growing up in Tulsa had made it a necessity to read S.E. Hinton's book *The Outsiders*.

"You writing about your trip?" the guy in charge asked me, still smiling. I was looser now, as these guys were clearly not going to harass me any further.

"Yeah, maybe. I have a contributor column on *Forbes*, and I co-wrote a little book last year with my buddy in Bozeman who I just came from seeing. He and his fiancée had a baby nine weeks ago, so I got to see them and meet their baby. Look, we were just tired of driving tonight and thought this was BLM land."

The less-in-charge officer looked at his watch. "You said you were just planning to stay a few hours...When I hear a few hours, I think four or five hours or so. It's 11 p.m. now, so that would mean you're planning to leave around 4 a.m.? Probably better you don't try backing this thing out while it's still dark, you know."

"Yeah, no, I was thinking of getting up around 8 a.m. and having coffee and bacon and taking my time a little."

They both laughed again, like they might do the same in my shoes. They were leading the conversation so that they could get out of there.

The guy in charge spoke back up: "Have you been drinking tonight?"

"Yeah, I've had a few beers."

"Okay, so if you've been drinking, you shouldn't drive this thing anywhere tonight. Just read the signs before you park on any day-use fishing sites from now on, okay?"

"Yes sir."

And like that, they were gone.

I went back inside, and Ty looked at me and said, "What happened?"

"Nothing. They said we weren't supposed to park here but just that we have to leave in the morning."

I lay back down next to Ty, ready to put the movie back on.

She laid her head on my shoulder and lightly said with her eyes closed, "I'm glad they didn't show up five minutes earlier."

GARDEN OF 1,000 BUDDHAS

THOUGH I MENTIONED TO THE OFFICERS THAT I WAS inspired to take the trip because of Steinbeck's book, I honestly hadn't thought at all about writing along the way or about the journey until they asked. I had been in a rut those past few months and let procrastination and anxiety get in my way. I hadn't even written any articles in months. When we woke up the next morning by that gorgeous and secluded river, I felt more energetic and enthusiastic about life.

My motivations for the trip weren't to get to know people or learn anything specific about our society in the process. It was more of a way for me to reflect, and about getting to know myself and having time to spend in nature with Hafa and people like my brother and Nic, and now Ty.

We were on the road 60 years after Steinbeck's famous trip, and the homogenization of communities had only gotten exponentially more widespread since then. Any sense of localness that was left in the 1960 version of America has all but evaporated.

There are some small towns and communities, like Clinton, where everyone knows each other, and they support each other, and there isn't a Subway or a Cheesecake Factory yet. But we all watch and read the same news on the same devices and from the same few media companies. We're all using the same phones and search engines and social media sites. And there are obviously more park regulations, day-use-only spots and crowded campgrounds with little privacy, dogs must be on leashes and everything is fenced in, in one way or another. In 1960, I suspect that one could likely park where one wanted and do what one pleased much more so than now. Today the crowds must be contained to prevent damage and littering. Lines up a trail to take that certain photograph to check off the certain scenic offerings along the way of the predetermined bucket list of attractions.

I enjoyed that secluded river that morning with Ty and Hafa in Clinton, Montana. You could sit in a lawn chair and listen to the flowing river and the birds and the sound of the wind, and really enjoy the moment. There was no traffic, or people, or lines, or fences, or sheriff's officers. The view that morning was well worth the minor, sudden interruption the night before. Ty and I made breakfast burritos that turned out incredible. We ate and then began packing up our home for the road ahead.

Once we were ready to leave, I moved the rocks from the fire pit back to where I'd found them. I carefully turned the rig around and headed back toward the road.

Buddha was once asked to reflect on his life, and his reply was that he's always at the beginning. Seeing as you can't change the past, accepting each day as "the beginning" without any preconceived notions or regrets makes sense. You can get a lot of things done if you view each day as a new beginning rather than a continuation of yesterday.

One of the apps on my phone suggested an attraction along our route called the Garden of 1,000 Buddhas, a place of which I was previously unaware. It's north of Missoula in a town called Arlee, Montana. Population 600. We got there early and spent a few hours exploring the grounds, which take up around ten acres. There were different sites and gardens, with the main one being a giant circle of 1,000 small Buddha statues, and in the center of the circle is a 24-foot-tall statue of Prajnaparamita, "The Great Mother," which could be interpreted as the "mother of Buddhas," the perfection of wisdom. Something like that.

Many of the statues had quotes underneath them, and you could feel a positive vibration of energy in those gardens, as lame or corny as that may sound. I don't pretend to know much about any one religion, but I believe in energy, and I could feel it in that area, walking along with Ty there in silence, enjoying the peace and design and care put into maintaining the grounds. There were only three other couples walking around the grounds that morning, so we had some space and took it all in at our own speed. The sky had clouds but there was only the feeling that a storm *might* come. Otherwise, the gardens presented us with a strange calm.

When we had finished exploring the gardens, we walked over to the gift shop to see if they had shirts or anything we could get to remember the occasion. When we walked into the gift shop, there was incense burning and every manner of Buddha ornaments, collectibles, clothing and books. There was a small Asian man working behind the counter who greeted us. Ty and I both picked out some shirts to buy, and I looked at the books. I picked one up and the man working there came and took the book from my hands and put it back where I'd gotten it from.

"Nah. Nah. This one you will not understand. Requires many weeks of teaching first." He was friendly in the way he said it, but I was still a little offended even if he was right. He then went on to explain to us how they had programs and retreats there at different times of the year, and that you needed the first 12-week training in order to start reading that particular book. Otherwise it wouldn't make sense. It was out of the question.

I pointed at some of the small pocket-sized books of quotations. "How about one of these; can I handle this?" I picked up *The Pocket Rumi* edited by Kabir Helminski.

"Yes, this is better." He nodded, made sure all the books were in order and even and then went back to his register.

He gave Ty more information on the classes and she

asked about the possibility of working or interning there sometime. Once everyone had everyone else's information, we paid for our memorabilia and walked back through the garden toward the RV.

Since this was a spiritual site, we'd made Hafa wait in the car. He was happy to see us when we came back and let him out in the parking lot to relieve himself, and then we were back on the road.

IDAHO

THE BUDDHAS AND ST. REGIS WERE THE TWO LAST stops in Montana. I didn't stop to check out Missoula, but I plan to some other time. Everything I've ever seen or done in Montana has made me absolutely love it there.

From Arlee, it was another 80 miles on I-90 West to St. Regis. Ty had made the trip from Coeur d'Alene to Bozeman many times, so she kept telling me how we needed to stop in St. Regis, Montana, population 319 people.

"There's this store there; it's like a big gas station with, like, a restaurant and they sell souvenirs and stuff."

"Sounds cool," I agreed, even though I didn't get what made that worth stopping there. She kept saying more about this place.

"Huckleberries are really common around here, and this place has the best huckleberry milkshakes in the world." She said it like it was a mic-drop-worthy comment.

I still didn't understand, but I also wasn't familiar with huckleberries, so I knew I needed to keep an open mind.

"All right, I guess we'll see."

"Yeah, on the highway you'll see almost every billboard on the way there on both sides is about the huckleberry milkshake. They have really amazing burgers too."

I'd had burgers at a handful of different bars and restaurants over the past weeks, but a famous shake and burger still sounded fine to me. And she was right about the billboards. Nearly every billboard I saw from then on either talked about this place and their milkshakes, or about another attraction called the World Famous 50,000 Silver Dollar Bar, which Ty said she'd seen as well, but we didn't need to stop there on this trip.

She went on about this all-in-one gift shop, restaurant and travel center. "They also have a big aquarium in the store that's filled with different kinds of trout."

"What? A trout aquarium? All right, well now I've got to see this place." The idea of an aquarium full of trout was and still is funny to me, but it's their state fish, so I guess there's a merit somewhere.

Within the hour, we pulled up and parked at the St. Regis Travel Center, and Ty was on point with everything she'd told me. When I walked in, I went straight to the back and found the aquarium. I thought it was cute that they advertise it as a "free trout aquarium" to let you know that you can make this a destination or rest stop to show your kids some trout, and it won't cost anything.

When I got to the aquarium, I found a young mother holding her young child's hand, pointing at different fish in the tank and teaching him, "See this? This one is a lake trout. See this one? It's a rainbow trout. Oh, hun, see this one? This is a bull trout."

I moved on and checked out the rest of the store. I picked up a few kinds of local hot sauce and some local seasonings for cooking. Ty picked out some lip balm by a local brand there that she liked, and we bought our items and moved to the food portion of the stop. The stuff I'd been promised.

There's a small restaurant inside the store called Huck's Grill. We sat at a booth; the place was nearly empty, with only one other table eating, and after five minutes or so I began looking around for someone to come take our order. There were two teenage girls working the kitchen and register, and one of them caught my eye as I was staring over the wall, obviously looking for some service.

After living in bigger cities for long enough, you can lose your small-town patience and cordiality. I'll usually act entitled to quick and flawless service, and this can rub people the wrong way when they're used to moving at their own small-town speed. When traveling, you should embrace the customs of the town you're in rather than righteous indignation about things being slightly different sometimes, as I needed to keep reminding myself. In retrospect, it always seems silly and outlandish. One of the girls mumbled to the other about how a customer was staring over the wall, wanting to order. I was basically waving them over, like, "Hey—I'm hungry over here!"

One of the girls finally walked over and took our order. We got two huckleberry shakes and two cheeseburgers. I added bacon to my burger, and we split an order of fries.

The food was incredible. Honestly one of the best cheeseburgers I've ever had in my life, which I promise is saying a lot. I'd had numerous cheeseburgers on this trip alone through Wyoming and Montana. This one was the best burger of the trip hands down, and the milkshake was a home run too. Since huckleberries seemed to be so popular there, I also went ahead and bought some huckleberry jelly to take home.

Ty was right about a lot of things, and I will say that it was indeed the best damn huckleberry shake I've ever had in my entire life, and one of the best burgers I've ever had too. We left, and I wondered how those two teenage girls working the grill were able to cook such a good hamburger.

COEUR D'ALENE, IDAHO

EARLY ON IN THE JOURNEY, WHEN MY BROTHER WAS still my co-pilot, we had discussed some of my future destinations, such as Idaho, and wondered what those places would bring. Neither of us had been to Idaho before.

Aaron told me that he'd heard great things, and posited, "As global warming continues, the hot and dry places will just keep getting hotter and dryer, and places like Idaho will probably start to look a lot more appealing to a lot of people. Like a hidden gem."

Aside from an occasional wildfire or mudslide, or a rare earthquake, those of us living in Southern California don't see too many extremes in terms of weather and don't consider the state of our planet much beyond our 70-degree sunny reality each day, so I think Aaron had a good point.

As we drove along, Ty told me more about her life and family, and we got to really know each other for the first time. She'd told her mom about the trip with me, but the plan was for her mom to pick her up in Coeur d'Alene and tell Ty's stepdad and stepsiblings that she had flown back home for a dentist appointment. The rest of the family didn't know about her saying yes to road trips with a strange man, and I didn't blame her mother for the cover-up. I even told Ty that while I loved her willingness to say yes and take a risk, even I thought she should be more careful in the future. Someday one of those guys with a crazy offer might actually be crazy after all. I was one of the rare few good ones, I assured her.

There were a few steep passes on the drive into the northern tip of Idaho, but the weather was nice again and the roads were easy to navigate. As we crossed the state line, I remember "American Kids" playing loudly on the speakers and both of us singing along to it. Playing loud music in the car and singing along feels like your own traveling party and much more fun than singing along elsewhere.

When I saw the sign that says, "Welcome to Idaho," we were winding a curve going up a pass, and there was a mountain behind the welcome sign, all during the magic hour of sunset, one of the most exquisite sunsets I've ever seen. I was driving and obviously couldn't take a picture, but a picture wouldn't have done it justice anyway. I still can't claim to have seen much of Idaho, but my entrance into the northern section was nothing short of majestic.

Coeur d'Alene is a charming city that feels like the setting of an 80s movie. The buildings are made from brick, and you can imagine the days past of a prominent timber industry in this sort of place. Population of 51,000. The city is built around a giant lake, and all of the homes I noticed had a middle-class sort of vibe, though I'll admit I didn't see all of the city. We picked out a campground on the outskirts of town, and by the time we got there it was already dark.

We parked the RV and went down to the welcome center to check in. There were a few other campers and RVs there, but they were spread out, and there were a lot of trees, so you still felt a sense of privacy.

The place was called Camp Coeur d'Alene. The campground is sort of built on a hill by the lake. Up the hill are the RV sites and probably 20 or so cabins. Closer to the water were the tent campsites, as well as a grassy area to walk dogs and a selection of canoes to utilize. I was sad that we would only have time for one night there, as I could imagine it being a relaxing place to spend a week. They even had a huge pile of free firewood for anyone's use just sitting there. It's far enough away from town to muffle the sound of cars and people, but it's close enough to go buy any supplies you'd need during the day.

When we walked into the building to check in, there was a woman around my age who had answered the phone when we called. There was a middle-aged guy working as well, but he was outside doing something, then he walked in the door behind us and introduced himself as Ron. Both of them were friendly, even though we were there well after closing time.

"Thanks for staying open late for us," I told them.

"Oh, no worries, we had to finish some things up anyways."

"I'm parked pretty close to a tree branch at our spot, and I'm not sure if I should open the slide."

"Okay, I'll run up there with you now and see. You're in spot 37, right?"

Ron and I walked up the hill to where I'd parked, and I left my credit card with Ty to handle the check-in logistics. Ron and I agreed that the branch was probably far enough away and that I could open the slide, but then Ron noticed that the power was shut off at that site and suggested that I pull forward to the next one. The place was pretty much empty, so I pulled up to another site and plugged into the electric there. I hit the brakes, lowered the jacks, opened the slides and grabbed a beer.

I stepped outside and kept talking to Ron while I hooked up the electric.

"So those cabins up there, they look nice. Do those have fireplaces?"

"They have fire pits outside. We're actually putting a lot of effort into improving some of them to book more *glamping* trips." Glamping was probably not as common in those parts even a few years ago, but my generation doesn't mind being pampered, including myself.

"Oh, that sounds nice; I'll have to come back here sometime. It's my first time in Idaho, and I love it so far. Really beautiful here."

Ron told me about how he'd actually grown up in California and had moved to Idaho about 15 years ago, and said it was the best decision he'd ever made. I looked around for the water spigot options to connect to the RV. The water tank is on the passenger side of the RV, but the spigot for my site was by the driver's side. I couldn't get it to reach with the tiny 10-foot hose, so I used the nozzle of the adjacent empty RV site instead.

"The water tank is over there, and for some reason I've got a small hose."

"Don't worry; I won't tell anyone." Ron was quick with that. I laughed and nodded in agreement.

When we went back to the reception area, the girls were showing each other dog pictures on their phones. The girl who worked there had a German shepherd as well, and Ty was sharing pictures she'd taken of Hafa along the trip.

After we'd all exchanged enough dog stories, we were given all the check-in info, and we went back to the RV to set up home for the night. I lit a candle, put some music on, grabbed another beer and went outside to sit on the picnic table with Hafa, typing away into the notes section of my phone as Ty went to take a shower at the camp's facilities. Something about her company and this place had made me start writing, and now I couldn't stop. Like love, writing conjures an emotion that you can't control or explain at all. Confidence came over me like a wave, all of a sudden and out of nowhere.

Something in a woman's touch can ease the mind but can't be explained in words. She'd cured my loneliness just like that. Call her a muse or whatever, but something registered. The last couple mornings with Ty I'd been sleeping in again, and sleeping well. I hadn't written in months, but here I was writing feverishly, struggling to tap the keyboard on my phone's screen fast enough. I wrote about the night before, our last stop in Clinton, Montana by the river and how the cops had barged in on us. I wrote about the Garden of 1,000 Buddhas and the huckleberry shakes we'd had in St. Regis. Ty came back from her shower and encouraged me to keep writing if it was flowing, so I did for a bit while she finished some classwork on her laptop.

Then I took a shower and started making dinner. She hadn't seen *Fast Times At Ridgemont High* before, so I put the DVD in and we watched it before going to bed.

"Now this is the most important, Rat. When it comes down to making out, whenever possible, put on side one of *Led Zeppelin IV*."

WASHINGTON

IN THE MORNING, TY MADE US SOME COFFEE, AND we went for a walk with Hafa to see the rest of the campground and the lake. If we'd had more weeks on the road, the campground in Coeur d'Alene would have been a really nice and relaxing place to stick around and unwind. As it happened, though, I only had another week of the RV rental, and I'd booked two nights at Mount Rainier starting that night. I was convinced that I needed to be on schedule for some possibly misguided reason, so it'd be another long day of driving. Right at 300 miles.

Ty's mom was at an IHOP waiting for her, so I drove the rig into the parking lot, and we said our goodbyes. I told her I was glad that she came along, and she said she was glad that she did too. Then, as quickly as she'd entered our world, she was gone with her mother in Coeur d'Alene, Idaho, and I was quickly back on the highway headed west with my dog. Hafa hopped back into the passenger seat and watched out the window to see where we were headed next.

MOUNT RAINIER

AFTER I DROPPED TY OFF WITH HER MOM, I KEPT driving on I-90 West, and drove straight through Spokane, Washington without stopping. I'd done some more writing when I woke up, and as I drove I felt the urge to keep writing more. I'd never really used speech to text on my phone to write anything, but I figured I would try it out, so I pulled up the notes section of my phone, popped in my AirPods, hit the microphone button on my phone and began speaking. It reminded me of the days when I was an assistant to a film producer, and I'd draft and send emails for him while he was on the phone with me. The emails would always end with a version of, "Dictated but not read, by RL." I thought about this while I yammered away into my phone's microphone, thinking of how it should end with, "Dictated but not read, by NP."

Sometimes an idea will come into my head and I'll forget about it before writing it down, so this new process was exciting to me. Despite talking in a low mumbling voice, I was still able to capture in the moment some things that would otherwise have popped into my head and then straight out of my often-unreliable memory. A lot of it was rambling garbage about my life, the type of stuff you'd be advised to tell a therapist. After about an hour of dictating various woes into my phone, I accidentally hit another button that changed the keypad into Portuguese, which made everything it was dictating show up in my notes in Portuguese, even though I was speaking in English. Even worse, the translation was garbled and most paragraphs turned into even more mindless muck than they were before.

When I last visited Brazil, a close friend of mine there, Monique, had enabled the Portuguese keyboard on my phone in order to use it more easily. I knew there was an easy fix to toggle between the languages on the keyboard, but I was driving and my attention was on the road, so I settled with whatever my phone decided to write, thinking that maybe I could translate it back at a later time. For miles, I continued to talk into my phone, and the words that it typed made no sense to anyone, especially those who speak Portuguese. Remembering why my keyboard even had the other language installed, I thought about and then dictated into my phone some old stories about Monique and the adventures we'd shared together. *Carol maior de drivers para...*

Hafa and I drove on toward the big mountain of Mount Rainier, the tallest active volcano in the United States. We buzzed the south of Seattle and came upon the park from the north. The campground I had booked, Mounthaven Resort, is about a mile south of the national park, so we crept through the entire park as the afternoon turned into evening. I didn't stop for gas even though I needed it. I just wanted to get there and park and relax. I was already missing Ty's company, and I wanted to put some of my bottled-up energy into doing some more writing.

The sun had decided to set while I was driving through Mount Rainier, and it was a spooky drive through twisting turns and steep, narrow corniches. The road would hug one side of a mountain cliff, curving around and up and up with no guardrails or barrier to keep you from driving straight over. They were the types of narrow cliff roads I'd had in my nightmares during the course of the trip. At times, I'd think about the trucker I'd met in the snow outside of Yellowstone, and how he said, "I don't stop; I drive for a living." That's how I needed to think. There's no time to waste; just keep moving. I was amazed at the staggering task it must have been to build these roads and tunnels.

Seeing as I was likely to arrive at the campground after-hours, I called ahead in my last moments of cell reception before entering the national park and asked them to leave my booking information by the check-in area under a floor mat. When I arrived it was already dark, and they had taped my information in an envelope to the door with my last name across it. Inside was a map and explanation for where my spot was and where the showers and laundry were. The pamphlet also said they'd been around since 1921.

There was only one other RV at the campground, and the rest of the place seemed pretty empty. There were some cute cabins, and it looked like maybe two of them were occupied. The larger cabin was in front of my campsite, and as I pulled around to back into my site, I saw two guys on the porch of the cabin doing crunches and sit-ups. My designated site was number 12, sandwiched between several huge trees that were impossible to see while backing in with a bus at night. I waved down one of the guys doing a front porch workout and asked him to help guide me in, which he did. I thanked him, and he went back to his cabin. I set up my site: set the brakes, lowered the jacks, opened the slides. Then I hooked up the power and emptied the tanks and let Hafa run around.

Each site had its own fire ring, and the wooded nature of Mount Rainier backed right up to our rig, allowing Hafa to go on exploring on his own like a jungle dog. It was quickly one of my favorite places. It felt like adventure there, especially since the place was nearly empty.

I took a shower, fed Hafa and had a beer. It'd been raining lightly ever since I arrived, and I was glad to have a spot to call home for the next couple days. I sat on the couch and stretched my neck for a minute and *crack crack crack*, things in my spine started popping and adjusting back where they wanted to be after the tension of driving the steep cliffs of my nightmares all day.

I could easily imagine going back and staying a week or two in Mounthaven at one of their cabins with a girlfriend one day. The big cabin in front of my site, with the two guys who were working out, had a Jacuzzi out front of it that really sounded nice. Since I'd been thinking about Monique, the remoteness of Mount Rainier and the nature and jungly feel reminded me of a cabin where I'd stayed with her in Cambará do Sul the year before. A romantic and lovely place called Parador Casa de Montanha that made for some real glamping. They'd had amazing views and Jacuzzis in front of their cabins as well, and it had been one of my favorite trips I'd ever taken. In some strange way, that campground on the outskirts of Mount Rainier felt like home.

The night was quiet there. I was low on groceries, so I made myself a quesadilla and some soup and watched *Spies Like Us* while responding to work emails with the camp's Wi-Fi. One of my favorite scenes ever is Chevy Chase and Dan Aykroyd going "Doctor. Doctor. Doctor..."

It kept raining, and I slept as hard as a dead man that night. Growing up in Oklahoma, I'd gotten used to the sounds of rainstorms and thunderstorms and had missed the rain the last ten years in LA. Most nights, I will even put on the audio of a rainstorm to fall asleep to. That wasn't needed in Washington.

We woke up on Mount Rainier, and it was still raining. Not pouring rain, merely a constant drizzle. I'd planned to stay another night there and do some writing and, if the rain let up, maybe some hiking. So I got some quarters, found the laundry, did two loads and took a shower. The RV had its own washing machine, but I wanted to conserve the propane in case I wanted to use the heater or take a hot shower. Then I cleaned up the camper a bit while listening to some Willie Nelson and the soothing sound of rain. I swept the floors, did the dishes, made more coffee and lit candles to make my traveling home a little homier again. In long days of travel, it's easy to let things pile up without hitting reset.

The managers of the place, a married couple named James and Zandy, were off-site, so Zandy sent over her sister-in-law to get me the quarters for the laundry. She and her husband were the occupants of the only other RV I'd spotted at the campground. I let Hafa out for a while to relieve himself and play fetch, then dried off his feet and put him back inside while I filled the rig with fresh water and finished the rest of my chores. I checked the oil in the engine; it was low, so I topped it off and then went back inside to check the rest of the emails I hadn't gotten to the night before.

When we were driving, Hafa seemed to accept his lack of activity and sat politely in the passenger seat. When parked and locked inside watching out the windows as it rained on a new mountain forest, though, he was excited and begging to go back out to explore. I cooked myself some bacon and eggs and then took him for a quick romp through a nearby trail off leash. Hafa had never explored a forest like that, and with a light rain it made the adventure feel even more off the beaten path. It was once again the best day of his life, and probably mine too.

We started down the trail, and I threw Hafa's ball off in the distance. He'd pick it up and carry it around, then get distracted and smell something, then get distracted again. Then we continued deeper into the forest, and he'd forget his ball somewhere, and I would tell him to "Round 'em up" while making a helicopter-type motion with my fingers overhead. Knowing what that signal meant, he'd begin sniffing and huffing like a K9 with a job to do rather than a silly pup bouncing around, and within moments he'd locate the ball faster than I could have ever found it. When Hafa's nose really gets going, he goes into a trancelike focus, with his quick, frantic breathing and seems like he is on the verge of a seizure. Being a city beach dog from eight weeks old, it was like Hafa had taken the red pill, seeing the real world for the first time and learning why dogs like to explore in the wild, and I felt like I was rediscovering some of the same things myself.

Going back to the park in Hermosa Beach would never compare to this. This is how a pup's first year should be; *this* is camping. In Wyoming, Hafa had seen snow for the first time, and in Washington he experienced real rain for the first time.

I folded my laundry and then handled some more work emails while I watched the movie *Clerks* by Kevin Smith. I'm sure glad he made that one in black and white. It's a real gem. Around 2 p.m., the rain let up, so I let Hafa explore the great national park in the backyard again while I did the same. We didn't get far that time before it started raining heavily again, so we went back inside, and I made some more coffee. There was Wi-Fi and power, and I was feeling more refreshed and productive. I did more work in Washington that day than I'd done on the entire trip. It had been months since I had written any articles for my column, and I wrote one in about two hours that day about how social media shouldn't show *like* counts.

Then I wrote about dogs and how important it is to train them correctly. I wrote about how I got Hafa at eight weeks old and had made it a point to pick him up like a baby every day, making him used to it and more submissive than some other dogs. The idea had sort of been inspired by my friend Zach, whose dad had cattle and would tell him the value of picking up baby cows every day. He said that if you pick up a calf every day from the day it's born, you'll eventually be able to lift up a 2,000-pound bull. My strategy wasn't really that I'd get my daily workout from this but that I'd have a polite and submissive city dog that wouldn't be at risk of hurting someone. So I make it a point to pick up Hafa like a baby every single day, even if only to show him that I can.

I watched *Clerks II* and then went to sleep.

OREGON

CRATER LAKE IS FAMOUS FOR BEING THE DEEPEST lake in the United States, at 2,000 feet deep, formed when volcano Mount Mazama collapsed 7,000 years ago. It sounds amazing, which is why I had it listed as a destination on the trip. My navigation told me I'd have to do 365 miles that day to get there, so Hafa and I did a quick morning hike and then left Mount Rainier early.

When I was packing us up to leave, I stepped on the edge of Hafa's water bowl and slipped and hit my head on the corner of the TV. Hafa's water bowl is big and metal and was nearly full at the time, so water splashed everywhere. I fell, resigned to the driver's seat, shouting obscenities angrily at the sky and causing Hafa to look scared that I may start hitting him or something near him. I calmed down and patted him on the head.

"It's okay, big dog."

We sailed along on the I-5 South. The traffic around

lunchtime in Portland slowed us for a few miles, but once we'd passed the city we were making good time again.

It was getting close to the end of October, which is when a lot of these parks close for the season. With the storms and snow, most of the roads leading to Crater Lake were shut down already, and I couldn't find anywhere on the map that made sense to camp out nearby. About 20 miles north of Crater Lake, though, there is Diamond Lake, where I could park. I'd told Hafa we were going to see the deepest lake in the country, but I figured he wouldn't know the difference or swim to the bottom to fact-check me. I decided that we would go to Diamond Lake, and I'd just tell him it was Crater Lake.

DIAMOND LAKE, OREGON

WE STOPPED IN CHEMULT, OREGON LOOKING FOR GAS and food. Chemult is a small community off Route 97 that has a population of 300 and is the type of place where they still pump your gas for you. It takes you back in time and reminds you of the type of human touch that used to be prevalent everywhere. It gives someone a job and provides a convenience for you. In an age where we outsource or automate every job we can, why don't we look to bring back jobs like this that provide a sense of community and convenience?

The gas station attendant recommended I try a taco stand nearby, so I walked over and got two tacos while he filled up the tank. I checked the roads on an app on my phone and devoured the tacos. I was close to Diamond Lake, so I called the recreation.gov site and asked if the campsite was still open. They informed me the campground was open until the 20th but much of the water was already shut off, since it was already the 18th. I had my own generator and full tanks of propane and water and was dying to get back off the grid on our own, so it sounded perfect. We hopped back on the road, turning around and taking a left where I would've taken a right if I were still heading toward Crater Lake.

When I pulled into the Diamond Lake campsite, everything was closed off except for one of the roads. No one working there and only one other camper in sight. I looked over the map and signs posted on a bulletin board near the entrance, but it was a map of the entire lake and wasn't helpful in navigating the campground itself. All the other info was removed in anticipation of ski season. I did a loop around the open road and picked a campsite a few over from the existing residents for the view of the lake. They had two RVs, a canopy and a fire going, but I didn't see the occupants.

After going for a short hike around the area with Hafa, I started a campfire and a small truck camper pulled up next to me. The man who came over was thin, late 60s with no discernible accent. He approached me, so I shook his hand to show friendliness and ease him about the German shepherd running circles around him.

"He's friendly!" I yelled as Hafa drew in to make sure the guy didn't defensively hit him or something.

"Say, I saw on the information board that there's hot showers here. You have any idea where that is? Gee, he's excited. How old is he?"

"He's about nine months, still a puppy. Been sitting in a car a lot, so he's happy to be here."

The man laughed as he petted Hafa. "It's okay, I like dogs."

"We just got here like an hour ago, but I'll bet I can find a campground map online."

It was clear that anyone could do this themselves, but he was grateful that I was handling the web search on his behalf. I found the campground map in about three seconds online and showed him where the bathrooms should be.

"Let me know how it is," I said. "A hot shower sounds nice. My name's Nathan, by the way."

He looked at me, surprised by the exchange of names. "Mike," he replied as he turned to go back to his truck. "What's your dog's name?"

"Raphael."

"Same as the ninja turtle?" He smiled, happy about my dog's name.

"Yeah, like the ninja turtle." He disappeared, and I assume he found the showers.

Diamond Lake, Oregon, seemed to be Hafa's favorite place ever. When we got there, he gradually got more and more excited, first romping around in the shallow end of the lake, and then later, after I'd made a campfire, continuing to run around the forested area near our campsite in circles—chasing birds, even though I kept reminding him that he'd never catch one.

For hours, Hafa took turns rotating between smelling for treasure, jumping in the water, running in circles after birds and picking up the same big stick and running around proudly with it, prancing more like a deer or rabbit than a German shepherd. It was, again, the best day of his life. Around 6 p.m. I had to nurture the fire to get it going stronger, then two more groups pulled through the campground. One in a sedan and another in a van. I assumed the sedan was a couple tent-camping for the weekend.

It'd nearly slipped my mind until then that it was a Friday. The Friday before, I had been out on a ranch in Billings, Montana with Nic and our dogs on 17,000 acres all to ourselves. The Friday before that, I was out on Sheep Bridge Road in Utah with my brother and no one else for as far as the eye could see. And there I was, on another Friday, in another nearly empty campground next to a big lake. Weekends spent like that diminish any feeling of missing out on big city gatherings or FOMO. Hafa didn't care what day it was; he was the happiest I've ever seen him, and that's all that mattered.

Then the sky cleared a bit, and the couple from the sedan walked by and waved. I waved back. As dusk settled, the entire area looked like a painting. My dog looked as though he was born to be there. The light wind caused ripples on the dark blue lake, with flocks of ducks floating to the east and the green conifer trees turning yellow for the season. It all made for a calming and unforgettable sunset.

"Yeah, this is the best day of my life too, big dog."

As Hafa dug up some rocks, I continued my attempt at getting this fire roaring. I had made over a dozen campfires on the trip at this point, but this one kept going out over and over again, and now it was lightly misting rain. I was determined to get the fire going. I spent two hours coaxing it to stay lit, and it wouldn't cooperate. Finally, after a prayer and some well-directed breathing at the fire, she stayed lit and became the campfire I knew she could be. Then about 20 minutes later, the rain came and, just like that, the fire was out.

I went inside and cooked a rib-eye steak. I rubbed it down with some black pepper and the seasoning I'd bought in St. Regis and cooked it on my cast-iron skillet with some butter and garlic. It came out a perfect medium rare with a great char around the edges. I tossed a few blue cheese crumbles over the steak, poured some whiskey in my glass and put on the DVD of *American Gangster* while I ate dinner. It was, without a doubt, the best steak I'd ever cooked. Something that we forget from the days of watching DVDs and VHS tapes is that people actually used to sit and watch trailers before movies. That's all but gone now, but I was reminded as I sat through all of 2007's releases while waiting for the title menu for *American Gangster*. Denzel is always great, and this time is no different.

On the other end of the spectrum, I thought about how Mike Judge's 1999 film *Office Space* hilariously touched on a number of aspects of American life and work routines of which Hafa was reminding me. There is a scene early on in that film where the main character goes to a group hypnotherapy session with his girlfriend since they are having some problems with their relationship. He tells the therapist that each day of his life is the worst day he's ever had up until that point. He explains how yesterday was the worst day of his life up until yesterday, and that today is now the worst day of his life, and that tomorrow will again undoubtedly be even worse.

I remember the first time I watched *Office Space* on a VHS tape in the den of my parents' home in Oklahoma shortly after it first came out. The picture encapsulated a time and place where corporate rules and capitalist-driven obligations were questioned out loud and juxtaposed with living a simpler life that actually makes you happy. And that line about how each progressive day could be your worst day struck a chord in me. At times in my life, I've been so foolish as to think that was even the case, naively wallowing in self-pity as though I were having the worst day of my life.

In a similar manner, I think it's possible that each new day can be the best day of your life, barring unforeseen tragedies or illnesses and other unfortunate circumstances. This mindset and the way I picture it is based more on feeling fulfilled than it is on some shortsighted hedonism, so don't get me wrong. It relies heavily on your own ability to be optimistic and focus more on gratitude than other feelings. There have been several periods in my life so far when I have expressed outwardly to friends and colleagues that each day was the best day of my life. They would ask how I was, and I would tell them, "It's the best day of my life," without any sense of sarcasm or doubt. And then the next day I would say the same thing and mean it just as much.

These periods were often times when I was in a happy relationship, excited and fulfilled with work and taking care of myself. And traveling. Some of the same things that make anyone realize their good fortune and live in gratitude. I don't pretend to imply that I am always quite so cheerful or cognizant of how lucky I am, but it can feel great to say that you're enjoying the best day of your life and truly mean it, and then to be able to say it again the next day. Hafa understood this instinctively, as I suspect many animals do.

SALEM, OREGON

OUR WAY OUT OF DIAMOND LAKE WAS LONG AND ICY. I woke up to Hafa rolling around on his back next to me, licking my face with his ears bent back submissively. I opened the door, and there was snow on the ground and heavy snow falling. It had happened again. I made coffee and packed out without a shower, thinking the same way I had at Yellowstone: that this weather would only get worse, so I should try getting south to California as quickly as possible. After about a mile of driving on icy, snow-covered roads, I saw a snowplow behind me and coming up fast. I pulled over to let him pass, then I followed up behind him in gratitude. I had 20 more miles on this road before hitting a major freeway, and being right behind a snowplow was the stuff of my dreams at this point.

I kept pace with the snowplow at about 40 mph until the road curved to the left and we came upon a recently overturned sedan in a ditch. It looked similar to the sedan of the couple I'd seen the night before, and the snowplow pulled over to go make sure the people inside had made it out safely. These icy roads are no joke. I had no room to pull over and assumed the snowplow driver handled saving people quite often, so I pressed on until the snow turned into rain.

On US-97 on my way back to the 5 South, the rain would let up for a while and then come down even harder. I stopped at a closed-down restaurant and motel to stretch and relax a bit from my tense, hunched over, snow-driving position and wondered if any people had moved into this defunct motel to squat. I peered into the windows of a few rooms to see small but cozy rooms with neatly made beds, all fitted with a microwave, mini-fridge and TV, and what I assumed was a bathroom. There was an old crashed Royal Navy plane parked out front, roughly signifying the lack of life at this place along a lonely highway.

To this point, I hadn't listened to or read any news on the whole trip, and I hadn't listened to any audiobooks or podcasts. Music had been driving me so far, but now that I was out of the snow and headed in the direction of home, I decided to listen to the audiobook of Anthony Bourdain's *Kitchen Confidential* as read by Bourdain himself, which a friend had recommended to me. I'll say that I finished all nine and a half hours of that audiobook while driving in Oregon. I knew of Bourdain and his show before, but I hadn't ever watched it or been particularly familiar with him. Once I started listening to him read his first book, I got obsessed and gained a whole new world of respect and admiration for who he was and how he viewed the world. Another tortured soul lost too soon.

The leaves throughout Oregon in mid-October range from a bright green to a dull orange, all the way to a deep maroon. All the evidence of fall was intensified by cloudy skies and drizzling rain and fog. Oregon is a place of natural beauty and eerie uncertainty. Based on the view from where we'd stayed the night before, it seemed like the sort of place where ghost stories could be true, and things could happen that you wouldn't expect in any other place. I hadn't stopped in Portland, and while I wanted to get to Eugene by the end of the day, the rain wouldn't let up, so I made a pit stop in Salem for another break.

I pulled off the highway and into a gas station. Salem is a decent-size city, at 173,000 people, so I had to maneuver between other cars to get to the gas pump. I bought gas and beer and asked for suggestions on finding a good grocery store. The guy behind me in line to buy gas pointed toward a grocery store across the street, so I went over to buy some soups and steaks and bottled waters.

Judy, the cashier, was old and as slow at scanning and bagging groceries as I am at doing statistics. But she was fun and talkative, and when she scanned my steaks she gasped at the price of $20 each.

"Woooweee, that's a lot," she said, then pointed at the labeling, "It's because it's Angus. This for dinner tonight?"

"Yes, ma'am, maybe," I told her.

I got back out to the rig, entered the navigation for

Eugene into my phone, and sat parked at the grocery store for a few minutes, thinking over my options. The rain picked up again, so I started searching for RV parks and campgrounds nearby instead of going on to Eugene. I had these steaks and some beer, so driving farther suddenly sounded like the wrong move. Within five more minutes, the rain started thundering down in a torrential pour, like it was hailing golf balls. All morning had been driving in snow, and most of the afternoon had been driving in rain.

After calling a few RV parks, I began worrying since they all seemed to be completely booked up. Finally, one of them told me they had a space available, so I hung up and drove straight over. To be honest, I did not explore much of Salem and am sure my experience there was hardly representative of the wonderful things they may have. My trip to Salem will not be your trip to Salem. And what I did see there was mostly quite depressing, to be frank. I drove straight to the park, which was near some freeway off-ramp in an industrial area behind a hardware store, in what I suspect was not the nicest part of town. I did pass a small lake that seemed close to the RV park, but it had a tall fence around it and had "Private Property" signs posted on the fence.

Most RV and tent sites I had stayed at so far were decent and intended for tourists and vagabonds to get out in nature and camp, but the place I chose in Salem was simply a trailer park. It was the only place within a city I'd stayed at on this whole trip, and it was an RV park where most of the trailers and rigs are there permanently. Not exactly the escape to nature I was in search of, but at least I could plug in and enjoy my steak and a movie in the rain and get some rest. When I checked in, there was an older woman working and a younger heavy-set guy covered in tattoos working alongside her. I suspect that they overcharged me, and I also suspect that they could have gotten me any drugs I wanted, had I asked.

The older woman handled my paperwork and the younger overweight guy with a shaved head and tattoos wrote down the Wi-Fi information for me.

I asked them, "That lake I passed, is that private property?"

"Yes, and you'd have to walk through a sea of tents to get there."

He then told me about another park within driving distance. Evidently there was a large swath of this trailer park that had permanent residents living in tents that backed up to the lake's fence.

"What if I walk around the way I came? I saw an opening in the fence; you don't think I'd get in any trouble being out there for 15 minutes with my dog, do you?"

The guy laughed. "No, I don't think any police will come by or bother you if you're just going to take the dog for a walk."

And so I agreed. I poured a beer into a paper coffee cup, plugged the RV in and locked it, and off we went to the lake. It was about a half-mile walk to get there, and the rain kept coming down harder and harder. We didn't have an umbrella, and I was in a thin denim jacket, but we'd both been sitting in a car all day, and Hafa and I were both willing to be cold and wet in order to explore a bit and get some exercise. We went through the opening in the gate and walked around the lake. I finished my beer quickly so it wouldn't fill up with rain. Hafa did his business and ran around a bit, and then we walked back. The RV park listed having laundry and showers, but this night I opted to use my bathroom and shower in the RV.

After I showered, I opened the awning and set up a lawn chair outside the rig to watch the rain and have a smoke and a drink. I watched some of the comings and goings of the neighborhood, but it was late and raining, and there wasn't much activity to speak of. I thought about how it would be a nice setting to read a little of a book, but I took out my phone and let it distract me instead with its infinite wonders. It's strange to think about times before cellphones, where if you were waiting for a plane or standing in line somewhere you may have read a book or actually talked to someone because those were your options. In my generation's lifetime, the tendency to do these things has vanished, and I'm as guilty as anyone. I stare at my phone so much. So so much.

Social media and endless apps provide a fleeting satisfaction for clicking and liking, and as soon as we scroll or swipe, the thought of what we just liked leaves our consciousness. Once we click *like*, we can then move on and forget it; we've done our part. Netflix can stand in for real human connection. Your smartphone can stand in as a best friend. We're likely raising generations of soft, materialistic, petty, self-absorbed worker bees with little ability to think deeply about a specific subject. Television helped destroy patience and critical thinking from one generation, and the internet has further weakened real human connections. I'd wager that if you read Ted Kaczynski's manifesto today about the second industrial revolution, he might not sound so crazy if you can overlook his gruesome deeds that got him his own media attention.

I wished I had pushed on to Eugene, but it was nice to at least rest for a while. A few days renting a house or a hotel in the nicer areas of Salem is a much different experience, I'm sure, but what I witnessed of Salem I didn't like, and I was excited to move on. This road trip was never meant to be spent in a trailer park, and I'm sure a similar situation in any other American city would have conjured similar emotions in me. Even still, I felt ready to leave that city as soon as I had parked.

No matter the city or state, I don't understand living in an area with such abundant land and then staking your place in the ground a dozen feet from someone else. I would prefer a hermit's life in a cabin by myself than anything like today's mobile-home parks and trailer parks for the same reason living in a building in New York with hundreds of other residents in cookie-cutter floor plans does not interest me in the slightest. Even in Montana, I had seen miles of open land followed by a small patched-in group of mobile homes in a trailer park, all crammed in together and surrounded by open land. Some of it could be that human beings are social creatures and like being around each other, but like everything, it's really mostly it's about money these days.

With a rising need for affordable housing, many families choose to live in a trailer park because it's in their budget range. According to the census, 6% of Americans live in trailer parks today. That's more than 20 million people. There is a nasty scheme of the 1% who buy these mobile-home parks in order to make small cosmetic renovations and increase their rent, driving people who are already struggling into even more hardship. There are many news articles about this nastiness that you can find, so I won't bore you with it here. John Oliver did a great segment on mobile homes too.

I was getting a bad taste in my mouth about it all, partially because it was the first place where I had stayed inside city limits during the trip and also because it was during the last few days of the journey. Perhaps it all simply reminded me of my impending return to LA, with its even worse traffic, pollution, homelessness, and other metropolitan misfortunes. The next morning, I packed out and left early. As I drove toward the highway, a bird flew in front of the RV and was instantly demolished. It seemed like it had committed suicide, as though even the birds didn't want to live there. I got back on I-5 South and drove toward California.

CALIFORNIA

YOSEMITE WAS THE ONLY DESTINATION LEFT ON MY list that I really wanted to see and show to Hafa. As none of my days were well planned, I considered possibly stopping in San Francisco for the night. I had friends there I could see for dinner or drinks. Or if I got tired, I figured I could find a place wherever I wanted to stop. The world was my oyster, at least now that I was out of Salem.

The weather kept following me, and for the first hour driving from Salem there were light flurries of snow dropping on the windshield. As I drove past Eugene, the weather cleared, the roads were back to what I was used to and we were going the speed limit again, finally. Diamond Lake had been one of the most incredible and beautiful places we'd been to, but after our stay the night before, I was ready to book it back to California. I only had the RV rental for a few more days, or else I surely would have taken the time to explore near Eugene and other parts of Oregon I'd heard so much about. The last three hours of driving through Oregon were extremely windy. I was better practiced now at steering the rig through wind, but it wasn't an easy task and my arms got tired.

We passed through the state line and went through the checkpoint to confirm we hadn't brought any of our own vegetation back to the state of California. Then, not far after you've crossed the state line going south on the 5, you go through a small town of 2,900 people called Weed, California. No joke. The town seems to have a tourism economy of people stopping through to buy T-shirts and knickknacks that say things like "I heart Weed, CA." Billboards leading into town make you want to stop and buy something cheesy, but I pressed onward.

In Redding, I stopped for gas. The gas station attendant was an older woman who I could tell had smoked too much in her life, or maybe just enough. Her voice was raspy, and she was irritable when I asked where the bathrooms were. When I went back to the RV and gassed up the rig, I looked up what food options were nearby. It was lunchtime, and I was hungry. I found a deli down the street and went for a sandwich to regroup and decide how much farther to go for the day. The place was called Dill's Deli & BBQ, and the sandwich I got was prodigious. It was called the Dirty Pig sandwich, and it was the type of sandwich I hope I would make and sell if I had such an opportunity.

There's also a town called Yolo, California. I was surprised and delighted by this name. It's a little south on the 5 from Redding. They have a population of 452 people enjoying Yolo. Hafa and I stopped on a side road near some farmland in Yolo, and I let him go run around and relieve himself. It'd been a long day on the road already, and we had a ways to go still. We hung out outside during the sunset. Now, I don't think I've ever seen a bad sunset, but I know a great one when I see it. The colors went from blue to purple and from pink to yellow, and with the landscape of farmland and a hint of an ocean breeze, it all let me know that I was nearing home.

We got back on the road and drove through Sacramento. We stayed on the highway, and as we drove through the city it was dark except for the city lights, buildings and cars. The traffic slowed down a bit but wasn't bad. When I got into the city, I decided to do something I hadn't done once on the entire trip: I turned on the radio to NPR and listened for a few minutes about an impending impeachment of Donald Trump. I endured it for about ten minutes before I shut the news back off and turned on some music. It was already disappointing enough that he was president that I didn't want to spend any extra time thinking about it or hearing how they'd decided that they wouldn't allow any witnesses at his forthcoming impeachment trial.

I'm not sure if anyone can really be objective about anything. Once a camera is pointed at someone and creates a frame, it leaves everything else out. The same people that likely hate Michael Moore probably haven't seen his movies, and they complain about how he only shows one side of a story.

Showing both sides of a news story is a contrived habit of our media to feign credibility. This would equate to the equivalent of a news anchor interviewing one scientist that believes in global warming and one that doesn't in order to show "both sides" with equal coverage, even though 99% of scientists believe global warming is real. Putting one of each on TV creates the impression for viewers that since there are two sides with equal airtime, they must be equally reliable arguments. Sometimes the truth is obvious, and the media makes it more convoluted. Americans elected a con man; we're still dealing with the consequences.

STOCKTON, CALIFORNIA

BY THE TIME WE WERE APPROACHING STOCKTON, I reckoned we'd already driven over 583 miles that day and were less than 100 miles from Yosemite. This would be a fair place to hunker down for the night, then get up early and go explore the forest. I'd called ahead to an RV park I found on one of my apps and suggested they leave my information under the floor mat at the registration office, as I was surely getting in after-hours.

The place I stayed at that night was called Windmill Cove Resort & Marina, and that night it was as though I was in a different world. They have some overnight spots near the marina, but there's another entrance to what I learned was a more permanent rental area. When I got to the camp in Stockton, the envelope with my name, map and paper to hang on the windshield were all there under the mat as promised. I didn't understand the map at all, so I drove toward where I saw another truck drive in, in search of my site to park at and set up.

So I went into the wrong entrance and drove around in what appeared to be the long-term rental area. There may have been 100 campers and RVs back there, and the road ended in a sort of cul-de-sac of nice motor homes. I pulled up to an empty spot near a dozen or so RVs that were parked facing each other like they were creating a huddle. These folks had barbecue grills and chairs outside, with Christmas lights strung around. It was bizarre, like I was having a psychedelic trip. I hopped out of the rig and found a lady wearing pajamas. No one else seemed to be outside in the whole place.

"Excuse me, I just checked in and have this map that says I'm in space number 11. I can't seem to find it, but there's an empty spot here. I'm just staying for one night; I'm thinking I should just park here for the night."

Choosing this open spot might mean I'd be her neighbor, so I handed her my map.

"No, this area is for long-term reservations. Like people and companies book it for months at a time. Yeah, the map has you circled over by the office. MP for Marina Point. There's a field back behind the office; you can just go there."

It seemed like she wanted to get rid of me, and I was suspicious about what I'd interrupted in their little community, but I followed her advice and went back the way I'd come. Sure enough, there was a field behind the main office where I'd gotten my map, so I went off the road and parked on some grass out by the powerline pole where they had an outlet for me to plug in. I set the brakes, lowered the jacks and opened the slides, then poured myself a beer and took Hafa out in the field. He sniffed around and relieved himself, then played fetch until he couldn't run anymore. It'd been a long day of driving for us both, and I wanted to have a real shower.

I packed a bag with a towel, clean clothes and some toiletries, then went off to find the camp's bathroom. I triple-checked to make sure that I had a towel. The showers there were the equivalent of a public park bathroom, as I'm sure it's used by the entire marina, and when I got inside I was relieved I'd worn flip-flops. There were no shelves to set things on, but there was a hook behind the door, so I hung my bag on the hook and turned on the water. Immediately I wished I'd showered in the rig instead, as the water from the shower smelled putrid, like a swamp filled with decaying leaves. My bag fell off the hook, and I quickly grabbed it and hung it back on the hook behind the door. I did a quick soap-down and rinse, and then my bag fell on the floor again, getting most of my things wet this time.

I turned off the shower, got dressed and went back to my home on wheels, defeated by that nasty shower. I needed a drink and a smoke to get the smell of rotten water out of my nose.

"Even for a horse, this wouldn't have been an adequate shower," I called at the bathrooms as I walked back to my rig.

As I walked home, there were sounds coming from the bar and grill down the road. Sounds of music playing, sounds of yelling and laughing drunk women who you could hear from a mile away. Then I got to the RV and saw a limousine drive past, going toward the bar and grill. I grabbed a beer, dropped off my bag, and fed Hafa, then went walking down the road toward the laughing and limousines.

It was easy to find the bar, as there were sounds of drunks audible from afar, and I just followed the noise. It wasn't as easy for me to find the front door, but I found some stairs and made my way into the upstairs bar from a side entrance. The place had maybe 75 people in it, but they sounded like 200 people. I took a seat at the bar. There were two mid-20s women bartending, both cute. I ordered a beer and looked around at the scene playing out.

"Hey, I'll have a Dos Equis. Is this a group event or something?"

The bartender seemed less than interested, but answered. "Yeah, they're here for a local high school reunion. Thirty-year reunion, I think."

The age of the crowd added up to what she'd said, along with the music choices the DJ was playing.

"Say, can you smoke over there?"

I'd noticed the other side of the bar was open to the outdoor deck, and there was a guy sitting over there smoking while sitting at the same bar that I was. It seemed unthinkable in this day and age.

"Yeah, of course." She shrugged like I was crazy.

So I took my beer and made my way to the deck and took a seat at the same bar, but outside. Ingenious. This sort of thing would never fly in LA. I lit up and nodded to the guy next to me. He was Mexican-American.

"Hey, how's it going? You a part of this reunion?" I asked him, though he looked like he was around my age.

"No, but people keep asking me that. They keep apologizing for not remembering my name, and I keep telling them I wasn't in their class." He laughed.

The DJ played some Beastie Boys, and there was a good portion of the crowd singing along, which made me happy, as I'm a big fan. Again, it was fitting for their reunion time period, and I didn't feel out of place. I spoke to the guy next to me for a while before introducing myself.

"My name's Nathan."

He shook my hand. "Nice to meet you; my name is Jesus. You live around here, or how did you find this place?"

"Oh, I've been on a road trip in an RV with my dog the last three weeks. We were just in the snow in Oregon this morning, and we're going to Yosemite tomorrow. I looked online for a place to park tonight, and this popped up."

"You were in Oregon this morning? In the snow? No way!"

"Yeah, man, in the snow. I'll show you some photos." I pulled out my phone and showed him a few photos of Hafa in some snow at Diamond Lake.

"Whoa, that's awesome. You made a good choice man; this place is really special. I come here all the time. Almost didn't come out tonight, but then decided at the last minute that I wanted to go have a beer, so I came."

"Yeah, same. I was tired from driving but figured it

would be good to get out and see what's going on around here. Is it usually this busy here?"

"Oh yeah, there's a lot of parties and stuff like this here, but this time of year is slow compared to the summer. You've got to come see the lake in the summer. Girls in bikinis, boats, beers. It's beautiful. Lots of people come here for the holidays, man. You should check it out."

"I'll have to come back then. This is my first time in Stockton. Today was actually my first time in Oregon too." I puffed on my cigar and was glad to have someone interesting to drink with after a long day of driving.

"Man, I wish I could do that. Just pack up and go on a road trip for a few weeks. My job, I can only get off two, maybe three days at a time." Then he told me about a girl in Mexico that he wanted to be with. "She wants to come up here and live with me and get married. So I'm working to save money, and I'll move her here and we'll get married, I guess. Since I was born in America, she could become a citizen and get a green card, and she's never been to the United States so she really wants to."

"Where did you meet her?"

"She lives in Ensenada with her family; we met down there when I was visiting."

"My two cents, if you want it, is you should have her come here for a year or two, get married and get the green card and all that. Then you should both move to Ensenada. She'll have gotten to see America and gotten it out of her system and might see why the simple life down there is actually better. You should still get married, but Ensenada should be the dream. Man, that's what I'd do, make a plan to end up somewhere like that. America isn't so great anymore. Look who's running it." I'd had several drinks by then, so I said it all to him very seriously.

Jesus and I at some point discovered that we were both the same age, 31. He seemed a little jealous that I was out traveling and he had to be at work in the morning.

"Well, you seem to be doing pretty well for yourself, for 31."

"So do you, Jesus. I'm not in any better position than you are. I just put the RV rental on a credit card so I could get out of town, but when I get back home I'll have to work my ass off again. You're probably doing better than I am, to be honest."

Jesus and I got drunk together and talked for a couple hours while the high school reunion played out around us. It might've been the alcohol, but at some point I started dispensing more and more advice to him.

I told him the story of the Mexican fisherman and the American businessman, then I passed on the advice a mentor of mine had once told me: "This guy used to always tell people when they were all down and out and depressed and broke that 'Tomorrow's another day' or 'Things can only go up from here' or 'It's only going to get better' but in recent years he'd learned better. And now he'd say, 'No matter where you are in life, no matter what happens, I promise you, things can *always, always* get worse.'"

We laughed, and I gave Jesus all sorts of advice as though I were the expert on such matters of relationships and life. I'm not sure if that was helpful to him, but I felt like we'd bonded, and I was ready to stagger out back home to my rig. We shook each other's hands and wished each other luck. I hope he married that girl and then moved down to Ensenada.

On my way out of the bar, I noticed some people from the reunion leaving in a limousine, explaining why I'd seen one earlier. I walked lazily back home down the gravel road. I went back to the Southwind and let Hafa out while I had one last beer. Then I put *Chinatown* on the DVD player and ate some Doritos on the couch. I watched about half of the movie and fell asleep.

The day had started in the snow for the first few hours, then rain for hours, then strong wind and by the time we parked it was the type of California weather we were used to. For the first time, I finally had a reason to pull out the fly swatter I had packed.

YOSEMITE NATIONAL PARK

HAFA AND I GOT UP, MADE BREAKFAST AND PLAYED fetch, then packed up and headed toward Yosemite. We left the Stockton RV park on a small bumpy road, and I was stretching my neck as I pulled out of the park. I stretched my neck down for a moment, then looked up to an angry man in a minivan honking and raising his arms at me as he drove toward me because I had drifted to the center of the road. I honked back and raised my own hands in response and moved the rig back over to the right lane so he could safely get by.

At one point on the road we passed a lake, and there was a big, impressive lake house on it that had a slide going from the upstairs balcony of the house all the way into the lake. I'd love to have a house with slides going into a lake or a pool like that someday. Aside from the inevitable wildfires, this seemed like an amazing place to live.

State Route 140 into Yosemite is a narrow and winding road through hills and valleys where you have to go 20 mph or so to crawl through, especially in a vehicle of that size. There were no guardrails, and I was grateful for my decision not to press on through this road in the dark of the night before. I dictated a few more paragraphs into my phone, which were again typed out in an illegibly garbled Portuguese. *Perfil simonal então não era leque*...Then I stopped on a hill to let Hafa out and take a picture. I again had no cellphone service and was excited to park soon to type out more thoughts I'd had while driving, but in a somewhat lucid English.

It was Sunday, and the RV was due back to its rightful owner on Tuesday morning, so I resolved to enjoy my last two nights with the same ambiguous itinerary that had brought us this far. I picked a campground nearby with hookups, laundry and showers on the south side of Yosemite so I could clean the RV and do some laundry one last time, and have Wi-Fi to finish some work and schedule emails to go out on Monday. I often work more hours on Sundays than I do on any other day of the week, and I schedule emails to send off to people all day on Monday automatically. Scheduling my emails would help ensure that business could move forward despite my absence or lack of connection the next day on any trails in Yosemite.

The place we stayed was a very nice park and campground called Yosemite RV Resort, but was similar to South

Campground in Zion where it feels like the other campers are right there camping with you because they're so close. There's a fenced area for dogs, but otherwise they have to be on leashes. When I got to the campground, I parked and went into the office to check in. The lady working behind the counter was sweet, but the price she gave me for one night was double the price of any other place I'd stayed at on the trip.

"We've stayed in Zion, Yellowstone, Mount Rainier, and Crater Lake, all in the last three weeks. And this is by far the most expensive place we've seen."

"Well, this is California," she said, and I remembered all at once what it's like to be in California. "This is an average rate for Yosemite and in this area. Things are more expensive in California." A truer and more arrogant phrase would be hard to come by.

"My dog and I live in California. Not causing a fuss, you can run the card. Just thought it was worth mentioning. Can we maybe get a site somewhere that isn't right next to someone else?"

She got us checked in and called for someone to show us down to our spot, which she said was the emptiest area available. One thing hasn't changed in the decades since Steinbeck: I observed a lot of families and even single men out there camping with their dogs, though most of them had small dogs that could fit into a purse or bag if needed. My last dog was a small poodle mix named Charlie, and he was a true gentleman and never once needed a leash. He always followed me blindly and faithfully to a fault, and only barked out of excitement when playing fetch.

There are many small dogs like that, so I don't want to generalize in my criticisms of small dogs and their owners. I notice, though, that when I walk Hafa at home, we often pass people walking small dogs, and Hafa looks and wags his tail, but politely keeps walking with me because he is trained, while the small dogs often bark and act angry at seeing Hafa. And nine out of ten of these times, while their dog is barking away, the owner will calmly say something like "Oh, sweetie, be quiet." Sometimes they speak to their dogs in this high-pitched baby-talk voice. It's funniest when these small dogs are pulling the leash with the owner following along in tow; who is really in charge there?

My dog trainer, Brian, said it this way: "Dogs understand green lights and red lights. They don't understand your command if you give it like a yellow light."

In my view, these people are encouraging their dogs to act like little barking devils because they never give them a red light and really tell them to stop. Being firm is never easy, but those of us with big dogs are more apt to give red lights and curb bad behavior because we have to. Gently asking them to stop barking will let the dog know it is really the one in charge, and a big German shepherd with no respect would likely become an issue at some point, while a yappy little 20-pound thing is, at worst, a minor annoyance.

There were a few small dogs at the campground at Yosemite, but they were of the well-behaved variety. I put

Hafa on his leash and inspected my campsite for a bit, trying to savor my last days on the road and in nature. I saw a few of my RV neighbors and waved and introduced them to Hafa. They were all sweet people and complimented Hafa on being so handsome.

I poured a beer into a paper coffee cup, grabbed a cigar and took Hafa to look around. We found the fenced area to play fetch with a tennis ball, and after days of long drives and not much running, he got tired fast. I put him back in the RV and fed him, started some laundry and went to take a shower. I remembered to bring my towel again, which meant I was finally getting the hang of all this.

Yosemite would be another great place to stay in a cabin or tent for a week or so, but like other RV campgrounds I had seen at other national parks, Yosemite had very little privacy. There were older couples and some families, many of whom I could see sitting at their campfire while I was sitting by my campfire. But it was the end of the journey, so I had settled for a place with a laundry, a decent shower and Wi-Fi to begin to clean up and prepare for the journey home.

Undoubtedly, parking off the grid on BLM land or at an empty campground, park or ranch is a much more special experience. Sixty years ago, you could set up camp nearly anywhere. Now it's all protected, regulated and monetized.

If it hadn't been for environmentalists like Edward Abbey and John Muir, who paved the way for sustaining and preserving these lands, these places I had been so lucky to see would likely have all been destroyed by now for purposes of logging, building sprawling housing developments or some other capitalist-driven consumer rationales. Without such luminaries, there would be an abundance of businessmen and politicians who would be willing to destroy and pollute and profit from our open spaces in exchange for the almighty dollar.

I realized and appreciated that the rules about leashes and confined camping areas were all for the benefit of preservation and sharing these lands with future generations, and ultimately were rules for the greater good. The park employees I encountered were all great people who believe in this mission. But I still longed to experience these lands as our forefathers did. Like Will Rogers leading a cattle drive on horseback from Texas to San Francisco in his younger years, before the trail was replaced with fences and railroads and *advancement* of all kinds.

Today, even our preserved areas are amusement parks of sorts. Now you can even stay at a nice resort and spa and ride horses to the giant sequoias and play golf in the morning. Seriously. These days you're better off driving to Yosemite in a BMW and taking the prepackaged tour like that, and you'll get to take the same pictures from the same vistas as everyone else. I wouldn't be surprised to find a Subway or a Cheesecake Factory up there soon.

Hafa and I woke up early to go look at the big trees. I wasn't sure about making it back to the falls or the famous half dome, but I at least wanted Hafa to see some of the biggest trees in the country. I had been telling him about them all month, teasing him about how much he'd love them. We packed up the rig and started back toward the entrance of Yosemite at a slow crawl around 9 a.m.

Thanks to my navigator, I actually ended up taking the wrong road initially. I went up a narrow dirt road before someone told me I was going the wrong way and directed me to the park entrance. As I turned around there were two school buses full of children going in that direction, all staring at Hafa and me as we managed to find a way to pass them on the narrow one-way road. Hafa was sitting in the passenger seat, riding even taller than me, and all the kids were looking and pointing at him as we passed by.

When we got to the entrance gate to Yosemite, Hafa's excitement was as piqued as I've ever seen. He came to the driver's side window with me to greet the employee at the gate.

"Who's that?" he asked.

"This is Raphael; I promised to show him some big trees today."

"Ahhhhh. Sorry. Can't take a dog to see the big trees. Have to park and take the shuttle up there, and no dogs are allowed at all."

"He could at least see them from out the window, and we could drive by?"

"No, you could park and take the shuttle up there by yourself, but no dogs."

This was another expected letdown from our obsession

with national parks, and it didn't look like there was much easy parking for big vehicles.

"You could take him to the valley; there are some dog trails down there. It's about 35 miles that way," he added.

It was the last full day of our adventure, so I thanked the man, paid to enter the park and proceeded into Yosemite. I figured I could go to this "the valley" and let Hafa at least sniff around a bit before we headed back toward home. Just showing him this place from a window seemed unfair, and I thought the drive would be worthwhile. I had no interest in exploring sites without my buddy; he had been patiently waiting for the promised sequoias, and I wanted to at least find him a big tree to sniff in the same forest. I had told him that Diamond Lake was the deepest lake in the country, and he'd believed it. I was sure I could also find a big tree somewhere and convince Hafa that it was the biggest in the country.

So we pressed on to the valley, one of many cars doing this tour of the same sights and smells, looking to take pictures from the same trails and vistas. The Yosemite Valley ended up being a fine place for Hafa. We were able to take a simple 3.5-mile looped hike around the meadow, and we only passed three families along the way, so I kept him off leash for most of the walk. The first group was a man with his two young daughters. I put Hafa back on the leash right as the youngest one screamed and said while clutching her dad, "He has sharp teeth!"

The dad was unsurprised, telling her, "Yes...because he's a dog, sweetie."

I passed them and then passed a man with a camera taking pictures, and I then realized I had brought a nice camera of my own on this trip and only used it twice. My phone had been more convenient anytime I'd wanted a picture of something. Then we passed two sweet old ladies who complimented us on Hafa's coloring. Since I had been thinking of cameras, I asked the ladies to take a picture of Hafa and me with my phone. Then I let Hafa back off the leash, and we continued the trail in peace. Anytime he would get too far ahead, I would tell him to stay, and he behaved as a trained dog would. Then I would wave him on, and off he'd go.

There were many new smells there, and Hafa found several areas to do his business to let other animals know he'd been that way. We took our time, as I didn't know if there would be many other areas where he'd be free to go off leash after this. The weather was perfect that day, and we spent a few hours wandering around in Yosemite Valley.

Once we were back to the main hotel-and-visitor-center area of the valley, I gave Hafa some more water, and we resigned to set back south toward Los Angeles. It felt surreal that I had to return the RV by the next day. I wanted to stay and explore, but the responsible version of me said that we had to go back home, so I obeyed.

LOS ANGELES, CALIFORNIA

OUTSIDE OF YOSEMITE, I STOPPED FOR GAS. THERE was a young, attractive woman digging for bottles in all the garbage bins, putting them into a black trash bag. Then she climbed into a big truck that some guy was driving and tossed her bag of recyclables into the back of his truck. Probably off to the next gas station to find more bottles.

I typed in Hermosa Beach as the destination on my phone, and it was strange to be making my way back home. I technically had the RV for another day, but the rental would be due at 10 a.m., so I had no idea where I could park close enough to make that time in the morning and unpack. Traffic and parking would surely be worse in the morning than late evening. It seemed like I needed to go home now. Fuck. The last 281 miles. In this weather and this kind of terrain, it would be smooth sailing. So I started driving.

By lunchtime I needed gas, so I pulled off the highway

into a town called Selma, California. Population 23,000. I gassed up the rig and parked in a shopping center that had a handful of food options. Everything in sight was a chain restaurant or fast food. The American diner is now officially a Denny's and a Taco Bell and a Pizza Hut. Nothing seemed local, so I decided on the one I hadn't heard of before. It was a small sandwich chain that ended up basically being a worse version of Subway.

In the background of the place there was music lightly playing on the speakers, and it sounded like a broken record or a Bluetooth too far out of range, with a mix of static, silence and, every other second, a bit of music. Like torture if you really paid attention to it. There were three other customers sitting and eating their food, oblivious. I thought my brain would explode, and it seemed like I was the only person to even care. There were two young people working the place. A guy on the grill and a girl on the register, both in their early 20s. I asked her, "Do you hear that? Is something wrong with the music?"

The girl somehow hadn't noticed. She was completely clueless. "Oh, I hear it now."

She looked around briefly. I guessed she was new there and nervous and didn't know who or what controlled the music in this place; she wanted to get her shift over without incident, that's all. She looked at the guy on the grill, but he had on headphones and couldn't care less about the music situation.

"I feel like that would make my head explode playing

in the background all day," I told her, pointing at my head, then made an explosion sign with my hands. "I'll need a minute to decide what to order, if you want to..." I tried to suggest with my hands that she find a way to turn off the music or fix it.

I looked around. There was a couple sitting at a table waiting patiently for their order who didn't seem to mind the audio torture, and there was a big man in a booth eating alone with headphones on who didn't seem to care either. Was I making this all up? Did the idea of being back in civilization and on my way to LA cause me to be oversensitive to this after being out in nature for a few weeks? Surely not.

She kind of half-tried to look around for a solution but was too nervously awkward to do anything.

Then I told her, "I'll do the number 42 with a medium drink."

When she brought me my order, the music was still playing the same mix of broken audio, and I quickly carried my food out of there and back to the RV. I ate the sandwich in the parking lot and was pretty disappointed in the quality but not surprised. Back in society and not happy about it one bit so far.

When I got back on the highway, I only had another 200 miles to go. The traffic was now heavier than it'd been on the whole trip, and the drivers got steadily worse. In Southern California, bad drivers will dart in front of a big rig only to slow down a moment later as if they have no idea of the weight traveling behind them.

It's always struck me how people can behave so differently behind the wheel of a car than they would in any other situation. Driving somehow makes you feel like you're disconnected from people because you're in your own self-contained environment shielded from outside interests. Incidents of road rage, people yelling and screaming and flipping each other off is all too common in LA, in my experience. The same people, in face-to-face interactions, outside of the protective camouflage of their cars, would probably never have the audacity to behave that way. But in traffic, safe in the confines of your car, you can feel more anonymous and justified in being a jerk.

Online and on social media, it's easy to feel the same way. Some users will send hateful or hurtful comments and messages to others, projecting their own insecurities. People are much more anonymous online than they are in traffic, and this leads to a culture of trolls and hate speech against people who they would never treat so poorly face-to-face.

This bleeds into online dating as well, or dating in such a technological age in general. It's easier to block someone on your phone or ghost them than to have an uncomfortable conversation, or any conversation for that matter. You can regulate who has access to you and how in a totally strange, shallow and inhuman way. This leads to new generations with more perverse views on conflict and the constant reconstruction of their own safe spaces that are really echo chambers of their sheltered beliefs. I don't know the solution for these issues, as I'm as much of a victim as anyone. I've deleted posts that didn't receive enough love, and I've blocked people who I didn't want to confront, for one reason or another. Something about anonymity and perceived distance makes us less human, even if it does make us more *connected*. Hopefully mine will not be remembered as the generation that created and embraced being a flaky snowflake, unable to handle debate or conflict in person the way that our species has for millennia.

Another frustration in traveling back to LA on road trips is that in most towns and cities across America, you can go inside gas stations and use their restrooms. Virtually everywhere in this country, that's an allowed and expected behavior. That is, until you get near LA, and then suddenly none of the gas stations have public restrooms. Luckily, my rig had its own, but I always noticed that smug, indifferent attitude filling the air as soon as your right to urinate vanishes on the road. Also in LA, no one waves back. I'd been waving at truckers and motor homes and getting waved back at for several states, but not a single one once I approached my own city.

The road into LA from the north on the 99 is steep uphill for miles, with lines and lines of big rigs all in their own lane on the right, gradually climbing the big hill at around 40 mph. I pushed the RV up faster past the big rigs and rode hard until we finally passed the incline and then cruised down and down. The traffic wasn't bad, but drivers kept passing into my lane and then slowing down in front of me, tempting me to flash my floodlights. Instead I just drove like I should expect to drive in LA, assholes surrounded by more assholes. A return to true anonymity.

At Six Flags Magic Mountain, I stopped at one last gas station and walked Hafa to some nearby grass before buying a cold coffee and a premade smoothie, one of the popular brands they sell in gas stations, nothing special. The parking lot smelled like we were in the city again. Then we got back in the rig and rode farther south.

Once I merged onto the 405, I turned off the navigation. The 405 South would take me to the Manhattan Beach exit and from there to my home, where I could unload my things before returning the RV to OB's house in Long Beach. I knew where I was now, and the cold coffee had done its job. We sailed through Sunset Boulevard and didn't have much traffic until Culver City, where we got a few minutes of the infamous 405 standstill, at 10 p.m. on a Monday in late October. All par for the course. Around La Tijera Boulevard the traffic lightened again, and then we made it easily back home.

I double-parked in front of my house and quickly brought some cardboard boxes into the RV, filled them with my supplies and carried them all back into my home. I unpacked the skis, the guitar, my wardrobe, groceries and all other manner of things I'd originally deemed necessary to bring. It was warm out, and I was sweating from the sudden jolt of labor. I opened the windows of my house, as it was stuffy and stale inside. It'd been over three weeks since the house had been last occupied, but a friend of mine had watered the plants and brought my packages and mail inside for me. I piled my things on top of my bed and dining table, knowing I would have to unpack it all later.

Once my stuff was all back in my house and I'd fed Hafa and had a moment to breathe, I loaded myself back into the rig to return the Southwind to its own home. My shift had ended as the rig's temporary captain. I left Hafa at my house, and although I had the same music and the same roads on the way to Long Beach, the RV now felt empty without Hafa sitting in the passenger seat in the co-pilot role that he'd served so effortlessly up until that point. I realized then how silly it was that I had been lonely a few times during the trip, since Hafa had never expressed loneliness. He had my constant company and new adventures every day, and he was thrilled about that arrangement as far as I could tell. But I had, at times, been an ungrateful and whiny peach.

I arrived and handed over the wheel back to OB, who expertly parked the rig in his backyard. I needed to open the bedroom slide in order to unpack the rest of my things from a drawer, since there hadn't been room while double parked in Hermosa to open it up. I offered him a beer from his fridge and told him about the things I'd broken in the RV: the handles to the propane and sewage tank and the sink cover. I told OB about some of the things I'd seen and the weather I'd driven through. I'd left him a treasure trove of fireworks to use with his kids, since there hadn't been any spots along the road where I could have legally fired them off. We talked for about half an hour, and then I called myself an Uber and went home.

THE END

EPILOGUE

THE NEXT MORNING, I GOT HAFA GROOMED AND cleaned him up for the first time in a month. I use one of those services where a van comes and parks outside your house and they bathe the dog for you right there. The service has a playful name, like Groomingdales. Then I went and got myself a haircut and grabbed some tacos on the pier with my friend Zach. There were people there meeting for business lunches, and someone behind me was pitching a guy for an investment in his startup and making an awful mess of it. I actually had to work to tune them out and not hear what a bad job he was doing at asking for money. The other guy got up and left at one point, showing that the pitch hadn't worked out.

Zach leaned over. "Man did you hear that? Worst business pitch ever."

"I was trying my best not to hear it."

"Didn't miss much. It was awful."

It was the end of October and 83 degrees and sunny

in Hermosa. People were biking and running, playing volleyball and surfing, and I was back to the picturesque and self-absorbed world of Southern California. I took Hafa for a walk around our block. That same block had once seemed so much larger. This little neighborhood had been the whole world as far as Hafa had known, but now he knew better. There's nothing like seeing the outside world to make you realize that your own surroundings have gotten too small.

And as we walked around the neighborhood we'd search for small patches of grass between the sidewalk and people's homes. Most times, there's either a small fence around the grass, or an obscene number of signs planted across the yard with phrases like "Keep Dogs Off Grass" or "Curb Your Dog" and even passive-aggressive ones that say "Please Be Respectful" and they've got a graphic of a pooping dog with a circle around it and a line through the circle. They don't have signs outside their homes about any other matter, only this issue of dogs fraternizing with their precious Kentucky bluegrass. You'll pass three or four homes in a row, all with their lawns plastered with such disgraceful garbage.

Please be respectful? I get, maybe, having one sign that says "Please Clean Up After Your Pet" or something, but most of my neighborhood seems intent on keeping their innocent, virgin grass from being peed on or disrespected and some houses will even have three or four of these signs splayed across the sidewalk on their lawn. The implication is, essentially, that if my dog takes an unauthorized dump in one of these short stretches of grass along the sidewalk, that I am basically looking around waiting for some dog-poop police to jump out and scream, "Freeze!"

There are some parks and areas where we can get away with playing fetch off leash for a while, but sooner or later a police officer will come up and tell me to put the leash back on Hafa. There were rules here in the city and we needed to keep our heads down and stay in our lane again.

Back when I first moved to LA and I worked as an assistant to RL, a film producer, we developed and pitched a handful of projects together, aside from the projects he'd developed on his own. One of them popped back into my head after I got home from the road trip. We had a show pitch from back in 2015 called *Pet Bucket List* about people taking their dogs on adventures. Some might be silly, such as taking a dog to a Michelin-star restaurant to eat expensive steak while wearing a bib, or maybe a dog hang gliding or surfing or hot air ballooning or enjoying a waterpark. Those types of things that you could imagine people sharing online.

Back home, I immediately reached out to RL, and we prepared a new pitch for the show and sent it to a few people. Who knows if we will ever get it made, but we're still trying. The theme of the show was never intended to focus on taking terminally ill dogs out for one last hurrah or anything, despite how bucket lists are generally thought of. It felt more in line with what Hafa and I had just experienced. We camped out in empty parks, huge ranches and day-use-only fishing spots. Hafa had gotten to truly explore and roam free and be a dog, all at less than nine months old. I had basically given Hafa a three-and-a-half-week crash course on how life should be enjoyed. I was proud about how I'd started Hafa's life with adventure so he would be more aware of the beauty of the world outside the city and the excitement of being on the road. Waiting until the end of a dog's life to show them a good time just seems cruel.

This is unfortunately the same way most people envision their own bucket lists, though: way off somewhere in the distance. In the present, we're too distracted and bogged down with excuses and rationale for why the status quo has to be maintained. My neighbor went right back to her complaining, and it seemed like I'd never left. OB claimed a disturbing amount of fees and damages to the RV on the rental website, which I tried to dispute, but when you're disputing electronically and an app is doing the arbitrating via email, the vehicle owner can apparently claim whatever they want to and prevail. So I was frivolously weaseled out of a lot more money there. I tried to tell myself, "It could be good; it could be bad."

Back at home, I watched a 1985 movie called *Lost In America*, directed by Albert Brooks, starring Albert Brooks and Julie Hagerty. They play a couple who are stuck in a rut, and both are unhappy with where they are in life; they decide to quit their jobs, sell their house, buy an RV and live off their nest egg, making the open road their home. They keep saying how they'd always dreamt of dropping out of society to find themselves. Once they're on the road, they quickly lose all their money and decide to park somewhere to try getting low-paying jobs to survive, and as soon as they've even barely tried that, they give up and go to New York City to beg for his job back.

That's how the movie ends. He takes his job back, with a 30% pay cut. They didn't even last two weeks on the road, and they went right back to the consumerist, capitalist rat race they claimed to hate. The movie ends there, but you know they were unhappy as a couple before they left and would surely be unhappy in that same monotonous situation again. For a comedy, it's really a depressing shit of an ending to me. The notion is, I assume, that you have to work hard and save up enough of a nest egg to travel someday later once you retire. And if you don't have that nest egg, you can't drop out of society and go find yourself. The open road is an illusion that's just out of reach unless you're rich enough.

But I don't really think that's true at all. People do it every day. They decide to work remotely, they travel cheaply, they cook their own meals instead of eating out. If you want to get on the open road, very little is stopping you. I'm a lazy American too. My habits are no better than yours; I know how to get in shape but often am too lazy to do anything about it. Sitting on the couch watching shows and ordering pizza is much easier, I know. Of course, it's easier to know what the right thing to do is than to actually do it.

When I succumb to my American-endorsed and

expected lethargy, I fall into the common tropes of convenience and safeness. Struggle is better for the mind than complacency, but still complacency remains for many of us, conforming our schedules as a way to pass time and keep a logical order to things without having to think about them.

Sometimes when you're in such a rut, digging your hole a little deeper can inspire you to find a way to dig out of that hole. Maybe that's the excuse, still. Regardless, choosing comfortable, quick and predictable is easier than choosing painful, arduous and unknown. We all know this. And we all know that saying yes to new things can be frightening, while pretending to be in control of your life by embracing order and routine feels much safer and more inviting.

When noticed, a meaningless routine should smack you right in the face like a brick, spew a rotten taste of boredom in your mouth and make you clench your teeth at the thought of living each day as though it were merely the same as any other. Letting your inner nomad wander and explore as it was meant to seems like the only logical choice, and yet at the same time too romantic a notion to actually achieve. We're taught to believe that we need stability and that we can wait until retirement to travel or be spontaneous. Personally, I would prefer the bipolar highs and lows of successes and failures to spending weeks and months in the same rut, going in circles to satisfy being accounted for at some dead-end nine-to-five job.

I rose early one morning. It was nice to be back near the ocean, and so I put on shorts and sunglasses and carried my paddleboard to the shore and pushed out into the water. I hadn't paddled in a long time, and so it took me a few minutes to balance and get my sea legs back. The sun was still coming up; there were only a handful of surfers outside and no other people walking on the beach yet. There were birds floating together on the water, some sort of common loon. It was as quiet and peaceful as I'd remembered it. For me, paddling has always been a form of meditation or yoga, as it clears my head and gives me a reason to unplug from my phone for an hour.

About fifteen minutes into my floating wandering, I was singing loudly, as no one was around or could hear. My go-to paddling accompaniment: belting out "That's Life" by Frank Sinatra. "I'll be back on top, back on top in June." After a few verses, I got tired and the waves were getting bigger, so I came back to shore and carried myself and the board back to my house.

On one hand I thought life should be about risks, but after three weeks or so on the road, I, like Albert Brooks in that movie, was back home too. I couldn't afford to keep the motor home rental any longer, and would have to go work hard and save more money in order to be able to go somewhere else again. The trap. Months went by, and I spent the holidays isolated alone. Back to a familiar territory of spending Thanksgiving and Christmas and New Year's all by myself and telling myself it's all no big deal. Like my dad and Jehovah's Witnesses not celebrating holidays at all, and instead saying they value each and every day. But that was all a mask for how I was really feeling, and the loneliness always eats at you more than anything.

In mid-February I decided I needed to go somewhere and get away again for a few days at least, and so I spontaneously spent a week in Iceland and London amidst a terrible winter cyclone. The whole trip was really a storm and a disaster in a number of ways that aren't worth going into here, including a near plane crash. When I came back home, I found that the Covid-19 virus was about to shut American life down for a while. In February we had already seen news of the spread from China into Italy and other portions of Europe. Many of the people I saw at the airport in London were already wearing masks, and I could tell that something significant was coming. I boarded my plane and went back home.

California was early to issue stay-at-home orders in mid-March of 2020. They even closed our beaches, so I spent that March isolated inside by myself again, thinking more about life and our silly idea of plans.

Once we were all ordered by the government to stay in our own homes and wear masks when going out for essential errands, the whole bucket list notion seemed even more pronounced. If you put off your dreams until retirement or some day in the future, you may be giving up on them. You never know what will happen or whether you'll be able to even leave the house again. Appreciating and respecting the moment we are in is the only answer. You never know when you need to live out your bucket list, so it might as well be right now, today. At the very least, you shouldn't be doing anything *every* day if you can help it. There's a good line about this by Tara Brach, where she says, "How you live today is how you live your life."

I wish I could say that I'd had a religious awakening of some sort on this trip, or that Tom Petty's spirit had convinced my mind to move on and that I could impart some lesson of greater meaning. But in the end, I still missed my ex-girlfriend and she still wanted nothing to do with me. Though if she had, I may never have written this.

Whatever sense of perspective or gratitude or renewed sense of optimism I had found while on the road had faded once I got back home. I was no longer distracted, but was still stuck in my own mind and I still needed to go through the day-to-day obligations to handle my business and pay bills and buy groceries. I was back in the routine just like everyone else. Right back where I'd started. But now because of the quarantine I wasn't even allowed to go to the beach. Bars and restaurants were forced to shutter, and social distancing became the new normal. With everyone now dealing with the same isolation, I realized that leaving town was, at its core, always about loneliness and loss, and my inability to deal with either. Escaping town works to distract you for a while, but after the trip, you get back home, and then what?

My road trip that October was never about the futile search for untouched nature or a desire to learn more about our culture. I'd been seeking peace and resolve and perspective, had found some, then lost it once back in the routines of home. I love living by the beach, but perhaps I've become disillusioned enough with LA to need to move to a new place and a different vibe, a different community. Ten years went by in a flash, and I remained stagnant. When I wake up each day, I yearn to be back on the road, traveling anywhere, and I know that Hafa feels the same urge. I'm sure that if an RV pulled up in front of our house and parked on the street in front of the living room window, Hafa would surely howl in enthusiasm and start bouncing around in circles.

That April, while in a pandemic-driven quarantine at home in LA, I set about the task of recounting all the details of my road trip that I could recall, thinking back to it and reliving a time when we were allowed to leave the house. You can never predict what you will find on the road, but it will always be interesting. Being locked in your own home is far from interesting.

While I write this, there is also a curfew in effect in most major American cities, due to both the protests and looting that have broken out. In late May, a black man named George Floyd was gruesomely murdered in front of a filming audience by a police officer in Minneapolis who put his knee on Floyd's neck for nearly nine minutes as other officers stood by. The video of this event, which included Floyd saying he couldn't breathe, sparked protests, some of which turned into riots and looting, with buildings on fire across the country. Our tensions have been up for a while, and the masses who were on lockdown and isolating for months are now out shoulder-to-shoulder, risking serious illness to protest police brutality, chanting lines like "Hands up, don't shoot" and "No justice, no peace!" The scenes across the country now include peaceful protestors being met with police in riot gear firing tear gas and rubber bullets into crowds indiscriminately.

With any luck, these protests will actually force some change and improve the methods of training police officers. Two hundred and forty-four years after this country's founding and racial discrimination remains an ugly reality that simmers below the surface along with so many other systemic societal issues. I'm not the only one that experienced loneliness or depression while being cooped up during the quarantine, and my problems pale in comparison to these sorts of bigger societal issues that oppress marginalized communities. I know that, and know that I have no experience or wisdom to speak to the plight of those protesting in the streets today, other than to listen to them and support them in some way.

Humans are social animals. We like to be around each other, and so any time of pandemic and mass quarantine leads to existential angst and trials of depression and fear. Compound that with economic depression and brutal and vicious police tactics in response to peaceful protests and people of color, and a powder keg in society went off and I suspect it will lead to changes for the better. Of course, I knew a guy who'd say, "It can always get worse." So it all becomes about how we look at our circumstances and how we pass the time. I decided to occupy my mind while isolated by writing about this trip and reliving the experience of being on the mostly free and open road of the American Northwest, more for my own personal escape than any other purpose.

Your own journey does not need to be like my journey. I share my experience only as a report from someone of my own persuasion and demographic dropping out of LA for a month to drive around in an RV with my dog because I was sad and disillusioned and lonely. I'm not an authority or expert on anything. John Steinbeck once wrote, "I set this matter down not to instruct others but to inform myself."

I think that is the case here in many ways, yet I also gravitate toward something my uncle Jerry once said: "The only thing to do with good advice is to pass it on. It is never any use to oneself."

My own advice, for what it's worth, is to live as if today is your last day on earth, and to live today as if you're going to live forever.

Ditado, mas não lido, por NP.

ABOUT THE AUTHOR

NATHAN PETTIJOHN is an author, talent manager, and entrepreneur. Nathan is a contributing writer for *Forbes* on topics relating to what business leaders need to know about innovations in media and technology. Nathan is also the coauthor of a short tactical guide, *Zen and the Art of Admin Tasks*, about outsourcing administrative work. In 2011, Nathan founded Corduroy, a digital strategy agency based in Los Angeles, where he serves as CEO.

Made in the USA
Las Vegas, NV
23 May 2021